PATTERNS

DRUSILLA COLE

LAURENCE KING

First published in 2007
This mini edition published in 2012
by Laurence King Publishing Ltd
361–373 City Road
London EC1V 1LR
www.laurenceking.com

A catalogue record for this book
is available from the British Library.

ISBN: 978 1 85669 885 6

Words and image selection: Drusilla Cole
Assistant editor: Caroline McNamara

Book design and cover illustration:
FL@33
www.flat33.com

Printed in China

PATTERNS

NEW SURFACE DESIGN

DRUSILLA COLE

LAURENCE KING PUBLISHING

ACKNOWLEDGEMENTS

I would like to extend my heartfelt thanks to all the contributing artists and designers who have made this project possible by donating their artwork so freely and helpfully.

I have really enjoyed doing the project and it has been a privilege to have been able to view all the lovely colours and patterns sent to me. I also very much enjoyed reading the comments, which were most enlightening and inspiring.

Many thanks, too, to Helen Evans and Susie May at Laurence King Publishing, Tomi and Agathe at FL@33, and Caroline McNamara for all their help and support.

Dru Cole

CONTENTS

INTRODUCTION

'Take any form you please and repeat it at regular intervals and, as surely as recurrent

sounds give rhythm or cadence, whether you want it or not, you have pattern.'

Lewis F. Day

This book is a collection of a number of contemporary surface patterns created between 2000 and 2005 by designers and artists from many different cultures and backgrounds.

The patterns have been achieved by a number of techniques, which include drawing, painting, collage, embroidery, appliqué, hand dyeing and screen printing. Many of the designs have been digitally manipulated. As this was a project facilitated almost entirely by e-mail and digitalized images, this is not surprising. What has been surprising is the range and variety of initiating ideas, as outlined by the artists themselves. These run from 'Mary Poppins Dissected' to 'The Cornish Seascape' to 'Chaos Theory'! I have included the artists' own comments on their inspiration and content wherever possible.

The patterns themselves have been chosen subjectively by me for their perceived qualities of beauty and balance, their use of colour and overall aesthetic appeal. They have been grouped into families following a contemporary understanding of the traditional surface design categories, and I have also arranged the patterns so that they fall in a definite and, I trust, pleasing colour order within each category.

CONVERSATIONAL
PATTERNS

'Art, by its nature, will always come up with surprises, and deals not so much with specifics

or with directions, as with overall patterns that must always be free to fall in fresh and

unexplored directions.'

Robert Butts

Conversational patterns are sometimes referred to as novelty prints and contain images of objects or situations. In these designs the artists' inspirations are not always immediately apparent until examined closely. For example, one series of wallpapers has been based on the song lyrics of Edith Piaf[1]. Other artists' designs are based on books[2], films[3] or even landscapes[4]. Some patterns in this section tell a story without words[5] or promote a point of view[6]. Also included here are patterns which contain repeating units of motifs which are similar but which differ sufficiently to give visual interest[7]. The inspiration for these motifs can be natural[8] or man-made[9] in origin. Occasionally, a designer uses the human form as a design element[10], or combines people with fantasy figures[11] and backgrounds[12].

[1] p.40

[2] p.13, p.57 (top)

[3] p.22 (left), p.56

[4] pp.54–55

[5] p.14 (bottom), p.50 (top)

[6] p.25, pp.38–39 (bottom)

[7] p.10, p.23

[8] p.32 (right)

[9] pp.26–27

[10] p.43, p.52 (top left)

[11] p.46 (bottom)

[12] p.44

Conversational Patterns

\ Giovanna Cellini _ Black cats, Siamese cats and tabby cats feature in this tight repeat, which is something of a novelty print. In surface pattern, cats are usually portrayed as fluffy kittens or as big cats and only rarely as th ey are here, as domestic pets. The artist comments: 'The idea for the print was to make it look quite regimented and a bit old fashioned.' **/ Giovanna Cellini** _ Naturalistic drawings of birds have been collaged into this design, which was inspired by the printed endpapers of craft books from the 1930s and 1940s.

012

Conversational Patterns

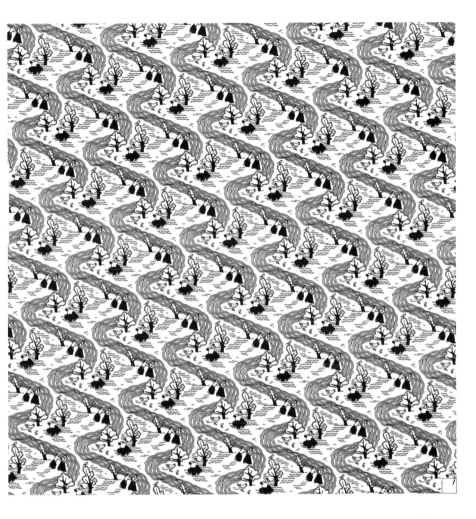

\ **Kim Barnett** _ A nautical themed repeat evokes a relaxed feeling of summer outings by the sea. The sails of the yachts have themselves been patterned by small designs of flowers and tiny boats. **/ Nadja Girod** _ Tiny figures in this pattern are engaged in Aikido martial arts practice, while being surrounded by flora and fauna in the countryside. The swirling lines of the rivers and fine details draw inspiration from Japanese woodblock printing. The artist comments: 'I was travelling in Morocco when I added the chicken and the rooster because I experienced that however deserted a landscape seems, there is always someone watching you. The bird on the top of the tree is supposed to be the bird from *The Wind-up Bird Chronicle* by Haruki Murakami.'

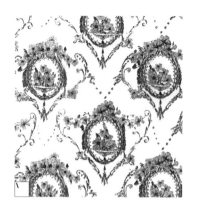

Conversational Patterns

\ **Rachel Moore** _ Reminiscent of early Victorian designs, with its swagged bowers and neo-rococo style, this design has the elegance of those times, but is contemporary in that its floral details are composed of halftone dots. \\ **Sue Westergaard** _ Faces drawn from a teenage magazine have here been placed on columns of flowers, symbolizing fruitfulness. The large X represents a kiss, presumably about to happen. / **Timorous Beasties** _ This is a contemporary take on the popular copperplate printed cloths or *toiles* of the eighteenth century. This version for a furnishing fabric takes a pastoral view of Glasgow and includes prominent landmarks and vistas, as well as citizens in stereotypical poses.

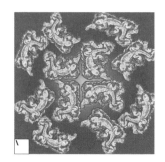

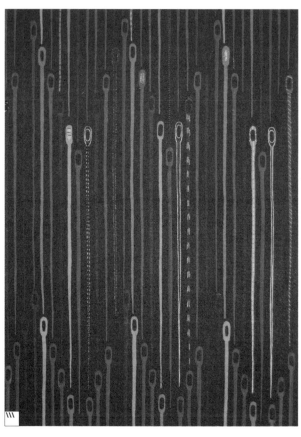

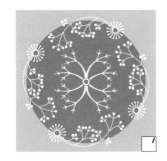

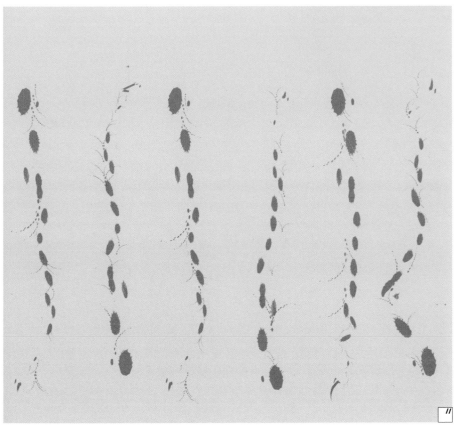

\ **Peggy Cole** _ Ice-encased lizards rotate around a light blue vortex in this digitally manipulated design for ceramic tiles. \\ **Frans Wesselman** _ An angel blowing his trumpet is depicted in this panel of stained and painted glass. The stylized leaves and berries use the brilliant blue and crimson, which only coloured glass can produce. The artist comments: 'For a little while now I have been preoccupied with angels. They are often creatures somewhat lacking in personality, so this one is an attempt to instil some attitude.' \\\ **Emily Anderson** _ Super-enlarged sewing needles are laid out in staggered rows in this hand screenprinted textile. / **Daniele de Batté** _ Stylized white flower and stem shapes are arranged over a circle of duck-egg blue in this design for a ceramic tile. // **Peter Uertz** _ Vertical lines of cut oval shapes have been enhanced with delicate traceries of dots in this unusual pattern.

018 Conversational Patterns

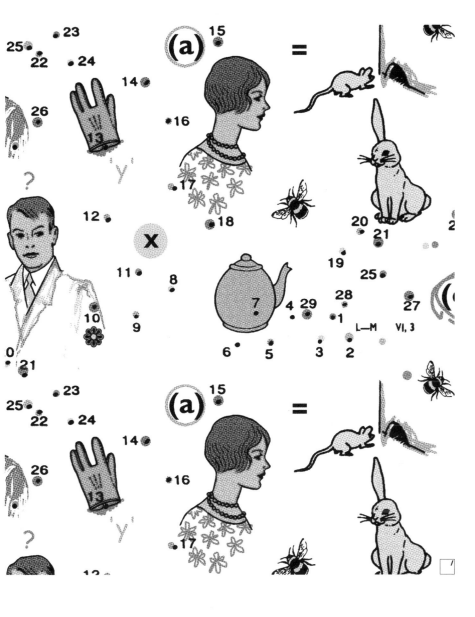

\ **Kristina Mörsdorf** _ Vertical lines of handwritten lyrics by Edith Piaf feature in this design. \\ **Kristina Mörsdorf** _ This pattern is part of a series of wallpapers based on the song texts of the celebrated French singer Edith Piaf. \\\ **Kristina Mörsdorf** _ Words scribbled across a blue background are lyrics by Edith Piaf, who became famous as 'The Sparrow of Paris'. / **Sue Westergaard** _ Brainteasers and 'join the dot' puzzles appear to be the inspiration for this design. Elements from each of these genres have been combined to produce this playful pattern.

Conversational Patterns

//

///

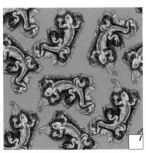

/

\ **Rachel Moore** _ A vibrantly coloured photomontage of contemporary buildings has been combined with floral imagery in this design for furnishings. **/ Dru Cole** _ Lizards crawl across a brightly coloured design for giftwrap, inspired by the work of the Victorian ceramicist William de Morgan. **// Dru Cole** _ Stylized horses parade in all directions in this design. Some have tiny ballerinas on their backs and others have coloured balls on their heads, suggesting they might be circus horses. **/// Carlene Edwards** _ Entitled 'Scaffolding', it is quite clear where the designer's inspiration for this design came from! It features poles criss-crossing over a background of sky blue, to produce a composed and balanced pattern.

Conversational Patterns

\ **The Church of London** _ Nautilus shells, anchors and a mass of other details make up this pattern inspired by Wes Anderson's film *The Life Aquatic with Steve Zissou*. The artist comments: 'I wanted the design to look like the inside cover of a battered old sea exploration book and have enough detail for you to discover new things every time you look at it.' \\ **Claire Perkins** _ Entitled 'Journey through a Hummingbird's Garden', this design includes typically Oriental motifs, such as pagodas and cherry blossom, interspersed with flocked details, which were added afterwards by hand. / **Gillian Tallentire** _ Emerald green surrounds these grey and white silhouettes of trees. The artist remarks: 'Taking inspiration from the village I live in and its surrounding countryside, I looked at trees found in the hedgerows and woods and used their basic shapes to digitally create this design.'

024

Conversational Patterns

/

\ **Aj Dimarucot** for **Collision-theory** _ Masklike faces, birds and a plethora of stylized motifs are combined in this rainbow-coloured digital design for fashion fabrics. **/ Carlene Edwards** _ Black and white photographs of a building and text from a newspaper form the basis of this design, entitled 'School Tables'. The artist comments: 'School Tables comes from the "City Living Collection" which is inspired by the visual and physical surroundings of my London borough of Hackney. I used a vibrant colour scheme to lift the whole piece and produce a bright pattern around everyday subject matter.'

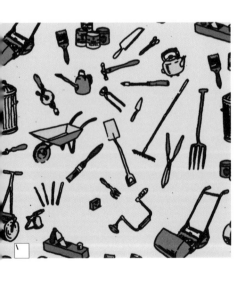

\ Emily Burningham _ The contents of a garden shed seem to have been the inspiration for this design. Old-fashioned carpentry tools, gardening equipment, paint pots and other bits and bobs are here depicted in an illustrative style, which evokes the magazines of the 1950s. **/ Kim Barnett** _ Tractors overlaid with coloured lines and interspersed with stylized flowers feature in this fabric design. It recalls the designs of post-revolutionary Russia when artists were encouraged to glamorize machinery and to produce designs based on the innate beauty of industrialization.

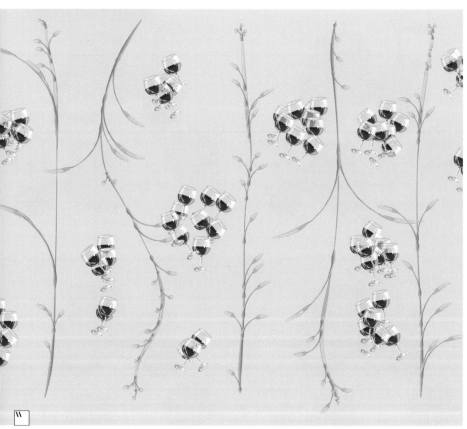

Conversational Patterns

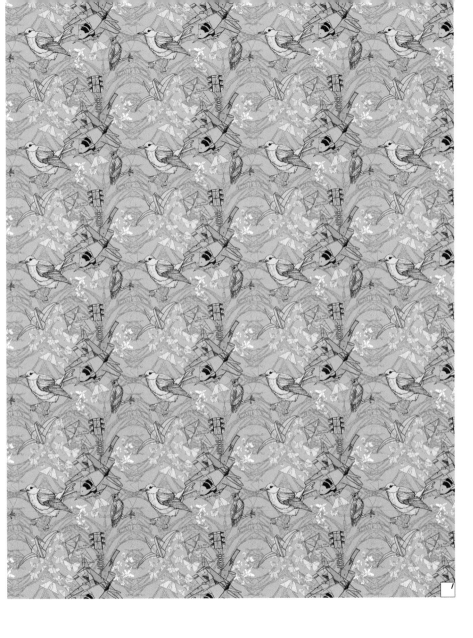

/

\ **Frans Wesselman** _ An allegorical design of a nymphlike figure and her admirer has been produced in stained glass and is a contemporary example of this ancient art. The artist comments: 'This piece is etched, painted, silver stained and kiln fired glass in lead. The original idea came from a poem by W. B. Yeats, "The Song of Wandering Aengus". In this commissioned piece a frog and apples have been added to make a link to the commissioner's organic orchard.' \\ **Peter Uertz** _ If you look closely you will see that glasses of wine have been introduced into this design as an alternative to flora and fauna. Cheers! / **Hanna Cottrell** _ The artist writes: 'This design is part of a series exploring the complexities of traditional Japanese origami, looking at the nature of the delicate folds that form paper structures, alongside investigating birds and the natural beauty of their wings.'

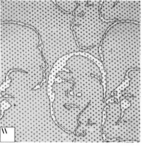

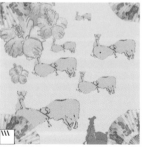

\ **Gina Pipet** _ Arabesques of blue and red, interspersed with ribbons and ballet shoes, feature in this design entitled 'Swan Lake'. \\ **Marloes Jongen** _ Contours of the faces of jazz singers, including those of celebrated artists Ella Fitzgerald and Louis Armstrong, make up this design. \\\ **Mary Daniel-Miller** _ Hibiscus flowers, fans and sketched outlines of cows are combined against a luminous yellow background in this curious design for a fashion fabric. **/ Sarah Devey** _ Two identical images have been digitally recoloured and overlaid with a traditional floral pattern. The artist comments: 'Inspired by images from my caravan holiday in Weston-super-Mare, this image is entitled "A Chintzy Holiday" as inside there are flowers all over the walls, the floor and everything!'

032

Conversational Patterns

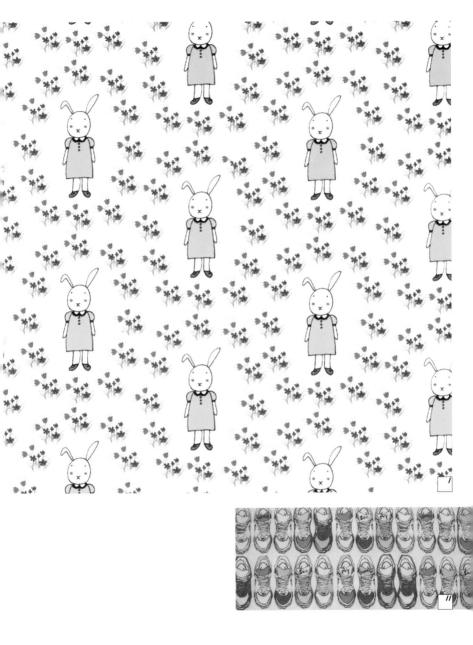

\ **Aj Dimarucot** for **Collision-theory** _ Japanese family crests, faces and flowers are combined in a complex design for fashion fabrics. \\ **Naori Priestly** _ Boy and girl rabbits, plus an assortment of flora and fauna, feature in this children's fabric. / **Naori Priestly** _ A cute girl bunny in a yellow pinafore, surrounded by a ring of flowers forms the repeat for this nursery fabric. // **Carlene Edwards** _ Neat rows of coloured training shoes form this design, which draws inspiration from Pop Art images. The artist comments: 'This design stems from youth culture and Hip Hop culture. I develop my personal drawings and photographs of trainers, DJ equipment and break dancers into repeat and placement designs for fashion. Trainers are a big part of street style in Hackney. These familiar shapes make for a great fashion print.'

 034 **Conversational Patterns**

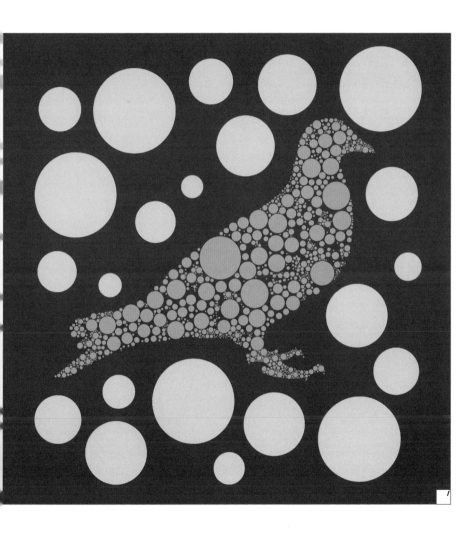

/

\ **Frans Wesselman** _ A swimmer is placed in the midst of repeating patterns of a shoal of fish and stylized leaf shapes, in this piece of painted, silver stained and kiln fired glass in lead. The artist comments: 'This piece came out of my own liking for swimming in open water, among the reeds, the fishes and the water birds. It is not a self-portrait; it is a distillation of the idea of swimming.' \\ **James Pegg** _ Grizzly bears are the unusual motifs in this screenprinted fabric sample. Bears are usually portrayed as cuddly 'teddy bears' rather than the real thing that the artist has shown in this pattern. **/ Daniele de Batté** _ Bubbles of aqua and cream against a brown background turn into a pattern of a dove in this design for a ceramic tile.

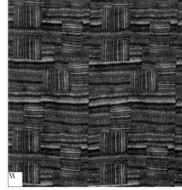

Conversational Patterns

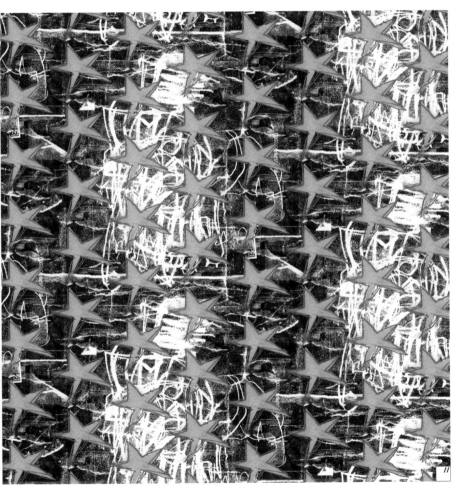

\ **Aj Dimarucot** for **Collision-Theory** _ A heady mixture of images of faces, birds and traditional Indian motifs has been digitally manipulated to produce this repeat. \\ **Kim Barnett** _ Knitted squares of multicoloured silk have been collaged into a design for digitally produced fabric. A favourite pastime of this artist, knitted items crop up regularly in her work. **/ Andrew Hardiman** for **Kuboaa** _ A single-colour large format wall covering, the artist comments: 'Designed to work as a more traditional pattern from afar, this resembles a typical trellis pattern. The trellis is made up of escalators with men on, travelling up through a jungle. It could be seen as a statement about man and the monotony of escalators and the everyday, but it is also designed to be a bit of fun really, and different from the other papers out there.' **// Alex Russell** _ Multiple scanned drawings of stars and scribbles are combined to give a design for fashion fabric.

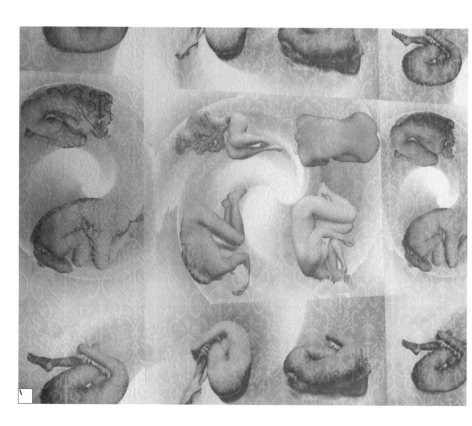

Conversational Patterns

\ **Dominic Crinson** _ Naked bodies of adults curl up in shell-like shapes, like sleeping, unborn babies, to form this extraordinary pattern. The artist comments: 'I like to use familiar objects in my designs; these could be as beautiful as the forms of the human body or as mundane as mushrooms. From here I emphasize and decontextualize the form by enlarging on a huge scale.' **/ Emily Alston** _ Origami paper planes and shadows of naturalistic birds feature in this wall covering. Birds have been a constant theme in surface pattern design over the years, especially on furnishing fabrics, where they bring a welcome element of nature to an interior. **// Emantras-India** _ The mangalsutra, a traditional pendant worn by married women in India, is placed in finely dotted circles and repeated in differing scales in this fashion fabric. The artist comments: 'A conventional design is used here as a pattern to break away from the traditional norms.'

Conversational Patterns

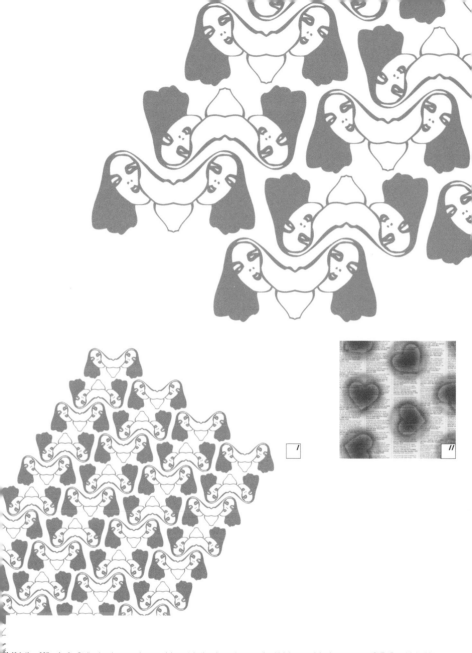

\ Kristina Mörsdorf _ Stylized arabesques in rose pink contain the phrase '*avec moi*', which is part of the famous song '*Si Tu Partais*', in this wallpaper design based on the lyrics of songs by Edith Piaf. **\\ Kristina Mörsdorf** _ Part of a series of wallpaper designs, this pattern combines handwritten lyrics from '*La Vie en Rose*', with classic French style and full-blown roses. **/ Jessie Whipple** _ Faces joined by abstract shapes form a 'turnover' or mirror repeat. This pattern is one of the 'Hermaphrodite Collection of Designs', which represent duality in both the flora and fauna worlds. **// Sue Westergaard** _ Personal columns of a paper have been airbrushed with heartshaped motifs to produce this design entitled 'Love Advert'.

\ **Peggy Cole** _ Vintage 'Reslo' microphones have been photographed and digitally manipulated in a simple repeat on an *ombré* or blended background. \\ **Darren Wilkinson Mawer** _ Appealing to those who enjoy a 'cuppa', this pattern features tea-related items on a bright scarlet background. / **Carina Lago Gonzales** _ Entitled 'Ice Cream', this hand screenprinted wallpaper features distorted images of a figure surrounded by strawberry pink and chocolate brown horizontal stripes.

\ **Naja Conrad-Hansen** _ Inspiration from glittery fashion magazines, old circus posters and stylized flora has been hand drawn and then combined digitally in this complex design for artwork on shoeboxes, which are to be marketed as 'Shoe Hotels'. **/ Cecilia Heffer** _ This heady mix of floral and abstract patterns was handprinted on to Shantung silk. The artist elaborates: 'This is a detail of a scarf commissioned by the Fashion and Textiles Department of the University of Technology, Sydney as a gift to the designer Zandra Rhodes. The idea was to reference work from previous UTS students' work and overlay them to create a new patterning.'

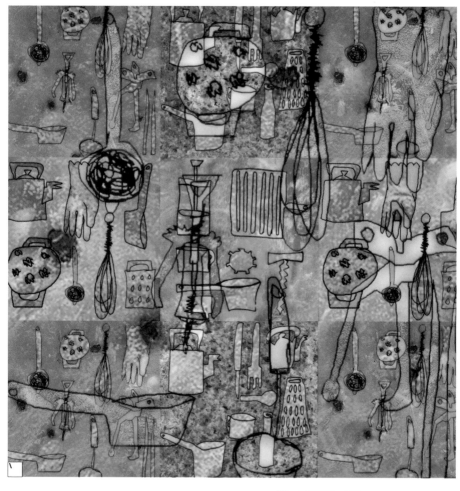

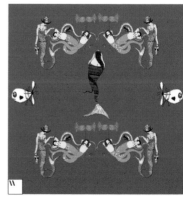

Conversational Patterns

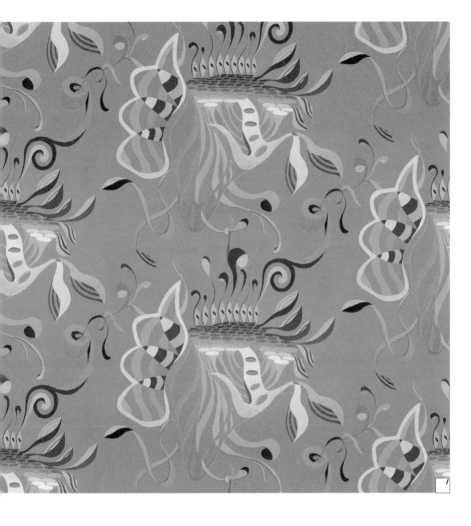

\ **Dominic Crinson** _ Household objects and kitchen equipment appear in this loosely sketched and brightly coloured design for digitally produced ceramic tiles. \\ **Kim Barnett** _ Fantasy figures of louche mermen, a mermaid and some frightened fish are arranged on a background of scarlet in this design. If you look closely you will see that the artist's favourite piece of knitting has made an appearance once again (see page 36, bottom). / **Gina Pipet** _ Drawing on influences from music halls and masked dances, this design features a lively miscellany of colours and shapes. The artist comments: 'Using inspiration from musical instruments alongside themes from grand costumes and plays, I hope to have created a pattern which is a real masquerade.'

Conversational Patterns

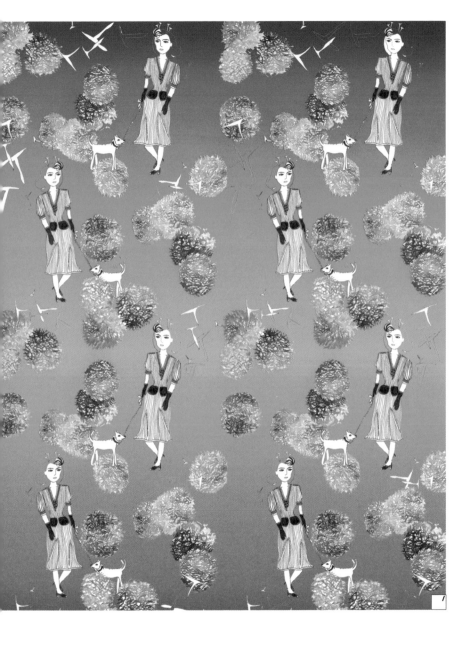

Sarah Devey _ In this digitally collaged design an Old English sheepdog is placed rather incongruously into a 1930s piece of embroidery depicting a typically English cottage garden. **\\ Emantras-India** _ White shapes based on the combination of crescents and circles are arranged on a ground of carmine red in this unusual design. The crescent has old associations with politics and mysticism, and is seldom used alone today; while the circle remains the most popular non-floral decorative motif. **/ Jiwon Jahng** _ Part of a series entitled 'Riddles of Similes', this handdrawn image of a girl with a dog is interspersed with painted pom-poms and has been digitally assembled into a design for fashion fabrics.

050 **Conversational Patterns**

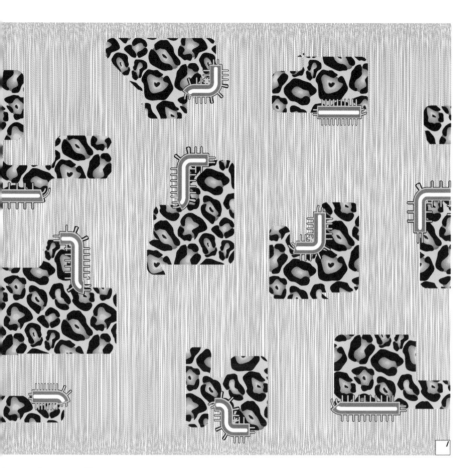

Rachel Moore _ Entitled 'Love Story', this graphic design for wallpaper taps into the romantic novels and magazines so avidly read by many. **Denise Boyle** _ Cartoon figures people this sample printed on pink corduroy in a design that is probably meant for kids but seems to appeal to the child in all of us. The artist comments: 'My illustrations were drawn with spiritual thoughts which project movement.' **/ Peter Uertz** _ Leopard skin patterns are arranged on a scribbled pink background to look rather like armchairs in this curious design. **// Timorous Beasties** _ Drawing inspiration from *toiles*, this design has a romantic ambience, accentuated by the delicate way the vignettes of London have been portrayed. The addition of birds – albeit pigeons – adds to the overall pastoral atmosphere being conjured up.

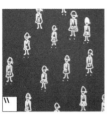

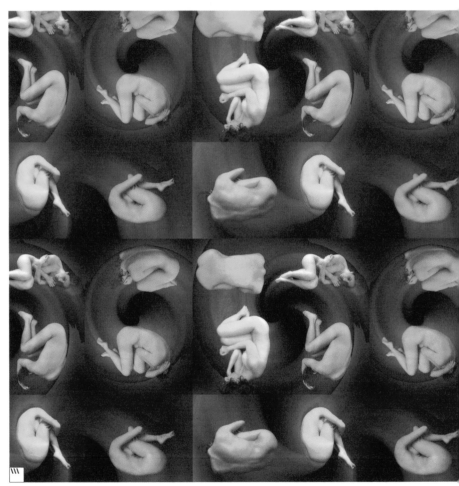

052

Conversational Patterns

\ Dru Cole _ Sirens portrayed on an antique Greek vase were the inspiration for this allover pattern. **\\ Anna Ostrat** _ Neatly pinafored ladies, with headscarves tied round their hair, parade in this design from Sweden. **\\\ Dominic Crinson** _ Wine coloured spirals containing naked human forms, spin in this strangely beautiful colourway of the 'BodyWall' pattern for wall coverings. The spirals leading into the depths add a cosy and distinctly womb-like atmosphere to the design. **/ Peggy Cole** _ Fader knobs and dials from a soundmixing desk are alternated with blue spirals in this pattern. The spiral form is a powerful and ancient decorative device found throughout nature – from the shells of snails and sea creatures to the arrangement of galaxies and nebulae floating in space.

Conversational Patterns

Erin Warriner _ The artist comments: 'I use classic imagery such as this rose from my garden which was placed within a charity shop picture frame. I manipulated the image to give a retro twist and a slightly quirky feel to a classic print.' **\\ Dominic Crinson** _ A montage of New York, based on photographs taken from the Empire State Building, is digitally printed on to ceramic tiles. The image is at once familiar and intriguing. **Sue Westergaard** _ Items of jewellery from a catalogue have been arranged into a simple repeat using a computer. Depictions of jewels of one sort or another have ornamented fabrics since ancient times – copying the practice of embellishing textiles with real gemstones.

\ **Jessie Whipple** _ The artist states: 'This pattern is one of a series entitled "The Sweetness of Glass", based upon the 1972 Fassbinder film *The Bitter Tears of Petra von Kant*. Using print as the visual narrative, the tale comes to life in a series of patterns which each represent one of the five scenes from the film.' **/ Jessie Whipple** _ Bold outlines of flowers, which turn out to contain booted legs, form the main motifs in this striking print. The artist comments: '"The Hermaphrodite Collection" is a series inspired by the book *Middlesex* by Jeffrey Eugenides. The designs represent duality in both the flora and fauna worlds.' **// Marie Hansen** _ Pegasus-style flying horses feature in this striking pattern. The horse is a symbol of power and strength, and the wings add a magical dimension, enhanced by the underlying delicate colour palette.

ABSTRACT PATTERNS

'Personally, my designs are greatly influenced by primitive art, microzoology, the natural

patterns formed by organic art and Picasso in all his periods, especially the stripy one.'

Eduardo Paolozzi

Abstract patterns are non-representational designs with freely drawn shapes and motifs, with no recognizable figurative or narrative element to the design. The designs included in this section have been inspired by themes as diverse as the patterning of tropical fish[1], the shapes string makes when stitched loosely on to paper[2], and the commercial advertisements and illustrations that form a background to many of our lives[3]. Several designs have been screenprinted to achieve unique and unusual colour combinations[4]. In a remarkable development, some patterns have been produced by the textiles themselves[5], using sound waves that interact with the metal from which the fabric is composed. Other designs have been created by seemingly unstructured sweeps of hot wax and dye[6] or by the swirling juxtaposition of different colours of molten glass[7].

[1] p.69 (top)

[2] p.61

[3] p.82 (bottom)

[4] p.82 (top right), p.85 (left)

[5] p.84

[6] p.80 (top)

[7] p.68 (left)

Abstract Patterns

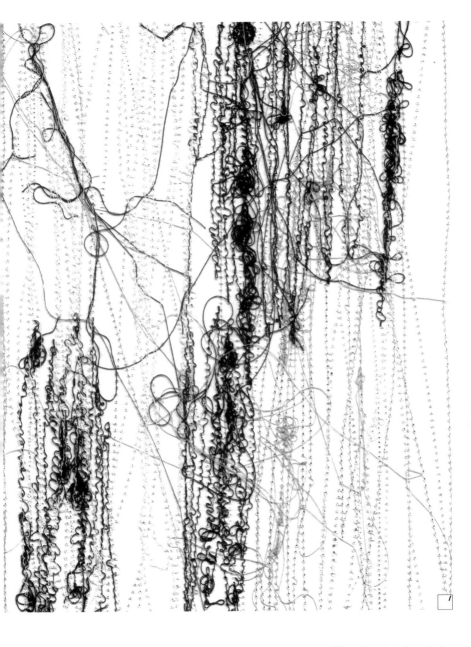

\ **Alex Eddison** _ Layered, undulating shapes have been drawn with a fine black pen. The artist comments: 'This hand drawn image from a sketch book was added to each morning as I commuted, looking to catch different moods through shape and placement. I believe the black and white areas of filled and unfilled space can create a very interesting subconscious pattern.' \\ **Emma Gray** _ Delicate strokes of blue create a large-scale design for inflatable wallpaper. It is reminiscent of Japanese ink paintings and was inspired by the blue and white porcelain of the nineteenth century. / **Rachael Taylor** _ Black threads stitched on to handmade paper were used to generate this machine-embroidered collage. The artist remarks: 'The sewing machine was used deliberately at an incorrect setting and tension level to achieve a loose knotted style.'

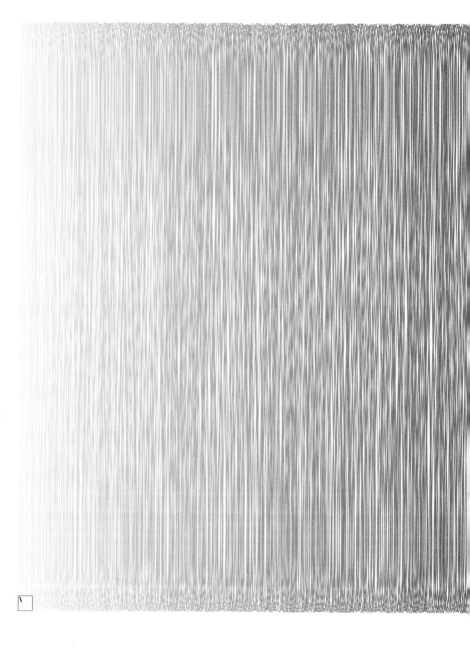

Abstract Patterns

\ **Peter Uertz** _ A blue background, blended from pale to dark, has been overlaid with finely scribbled lines in this unusual design. Also known as *ombré* or shadow patterns, blends are distinguished by a gradual shading and blending of the constituent colours. **/ Safa Maryam Taheri** _ Entitled 'Crazy', this blue and orange digital design has a distinctly three-dimensional appearance – almost like that of scrunched up multicoloured metal foil. **// Ed Jones** _ A generously proportioned area of blue, looking like the sky over a network of cranes, features in this screenprinted textile sample.

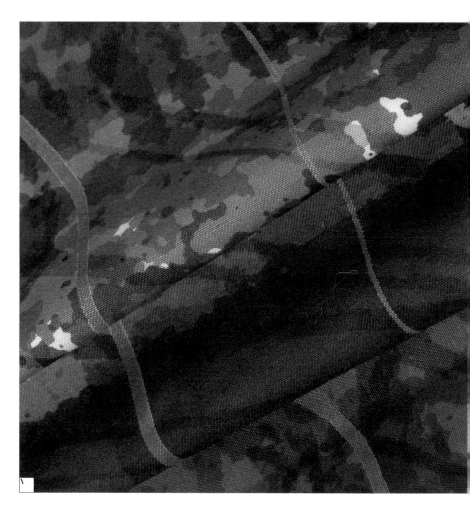

Ed Jones _ Brilliant blues and purples, juxtaposed with a thin red line, are printed all over these textiles to form a bold design. The abstract shapes of the patterns were inspired by magnified chalk lines. **/ Ed Jones** _ The artist comments: 'This development of a previous work uses composition to create more space and freedom for the red line to integrate.'

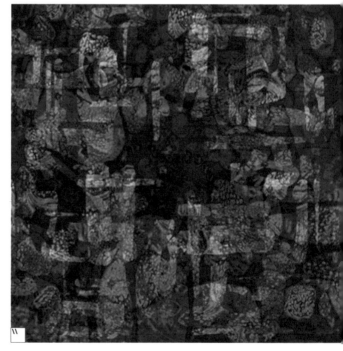

Abstract Patterns

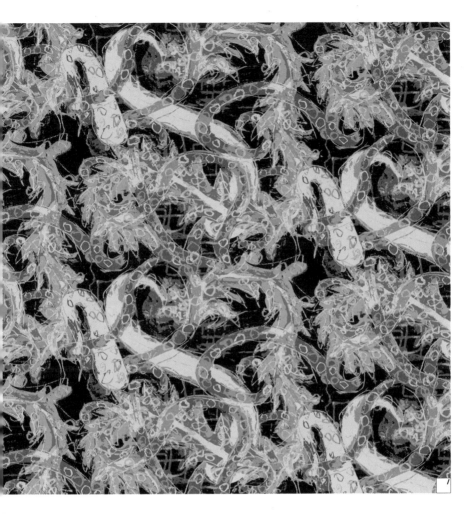

\ **Sara Sulemanji** _ A great sweep of iridescent colour makes this pattern resemble a breaking wave. The artist writes: 'This design is inspired by butterflies. I was particularly interested in capturing the rich, velvety colours, which contrast with flashes of bright luminous colour as the butterflies move through the air. The sample is a combination of screenprinting and hand painting using gold pigment on spun silk.' \\ **Louise Kallinicou** _ The sensitivity of the original collage has been retained in the complex image, which appears to rotate around a central vortex. The artist explains: 'Different layers have been rotated over each other to build up this four-way repeat. Certain layers vary in opacity in order to create the illusion of depth.' / **Alex Russell** _ Leaves and stems wind and writhe in profusion in this strikingly coloured pattern. The artist comments: 'Paintings, loosely based on traditional textile patterns, are digitally manipulated and coloured to produce a repeat design for fashion fabrics.'

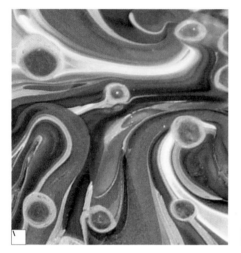

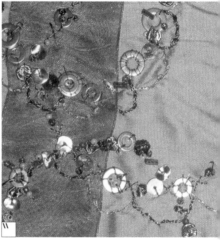

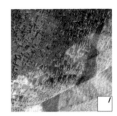

\ **Pauline Holt** for **Jazzy Lily Hot Glass** _ Swirling molten glass has formed this pattern. The artist comments: 'This is a handmade lampworked bead. The rich reds and golds are reminiscent of the colourful saris worn in the Indian State of Jaipur.' \\ **Donna Bailey** _ Buttons and beads have been sewn on by hand to make a fabric sample inspired by old dismantled watches. The artist remarks: 'I love the delicate and interesting shapes the fastenings and linkages of the mechanisms portray.' / **Sara Sulemanji** _ Watery tones and flecks of contrasting colours give these pieces of printed silk a feeling of movement and vivacity. The artist writes: 'This design is inspired by tropical fish and uses different print pastes, as well as pleating and folding techniques, to change its shape.' // **Caroline McNamara** _ Barcelona, one of the most photogenic of cities, was the inspiration for this digital pattern.

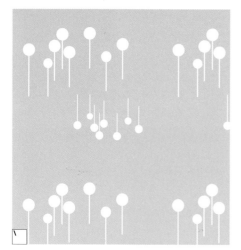

Abstract Patterns

\ **Emantras-India** _ The artist comments: 'These forms lend themselves to multiple interpretations. They are suggestive of popsicles, dancing abstract human forms, many yoyos springing into action and many more visuals as perceived in the mind's eye of the viewer.' \\ **Gina Pipet** _ Serpentine ribbon shapes float across this digital design in an animated manner. The artist remarks: 'This design was inspired by zoo life with its inhabitants; the animals and creatures. When creating this pattern an extremely intriguing form appeared of its own volition, suggestive of a somewhat mythical creature derived from zoo animals.' \\\ **Alex Russell** _ Angular shapes are combined with handpainted and computer-generated imagery in this fashion design. / **Lena Corwin** _ Entitled 'Village', the images on this pattern swirl and swoop in a frenzy of contour lines and whorls, which suggest the design was inspired by an aerial view.

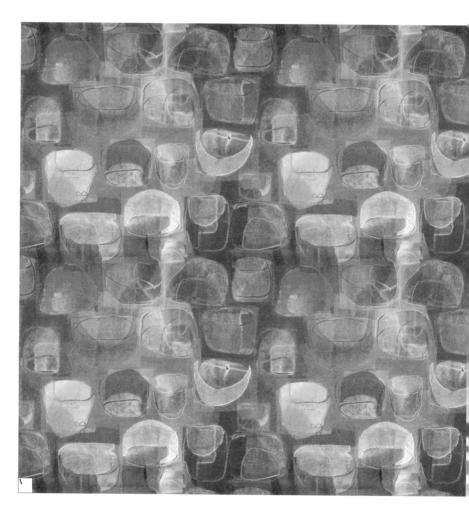

072

Abstract Patterns

\ Alex Russell _ Shades of green, orange and brown feature in this design derived from images of drawn and painted household objects. The chosen colours are restful on the eye, and the motifs intriguing. **/ Eugene Van Veldhoven** _ Textured cloudlike shapes on a ribbed fabric produce this unusual fabric sample. The artist makes these comments: 'On an ottoman fabric, a graphic design has been printed with expanding ink. The print is combined with a gold pearlescent acrylic coating.'

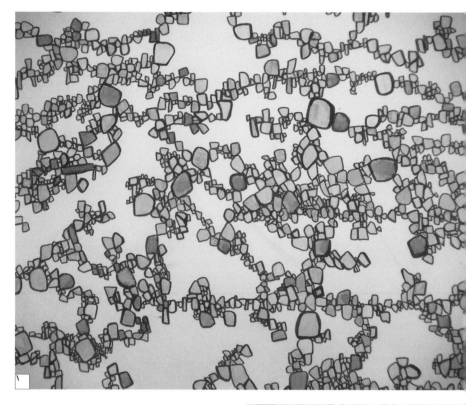

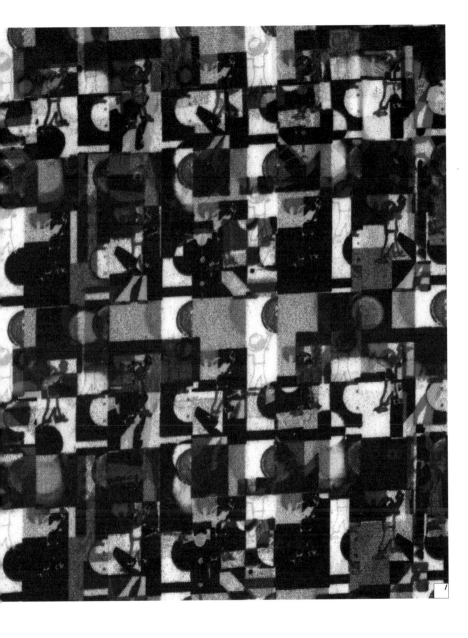

Suse Schröder _ Simplified discs of colour are linked together in strings and clusters to form this abstract design. **\\ Donna Bailey** _ Beaded circles of pastel coloured fabrics have been hand embroidered to produce this sample inspired by old watches which were dismantled for study. **Alex Eddison** _ Drawn and digitally manipulated images of Cornwall were the basis for this design. The artist comments: 'Some lovely patterned rocks I picked up on the beach were the starting point for this repeat pattern, which I layered and filtered, looking for a very graphic and contemporary feel.'

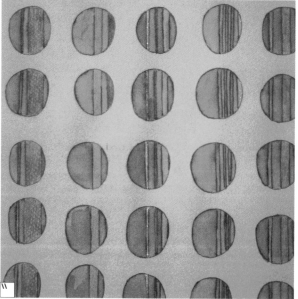

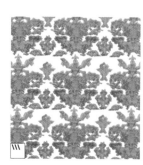

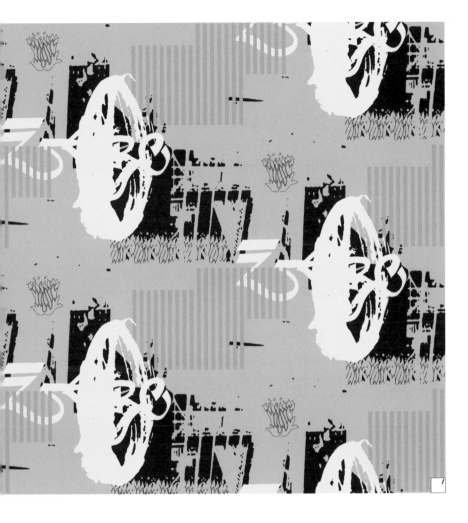

Veronica Pock _ This *in situ* photo depicts two wall coverings draped across a wooden floor. It clearly shows the mixture of luminosity and shadow that the appliquéd, baroque line of the pattern is designed to produce. This pattern is part of 'A Twist of Fate?' series, which explores the idea of chaos theory. **\\ Suse Schröder** _ Stripes of blue and brown can just about be seen through a net of circles in this hand-rendered design for fashion fabrics. **\\\ Timorous Beasties** _ Resembling a classic Renaissance textile, this design appears, on closer inspection, to be composed of a psychiatrist's ink blot! The result is an intriguing and unusual wall covering, here presented in shades of gold and bronze. **/ Alex Russell** _ The artist comments: 'Photographs, drawings, simple patterns and tags are mixed (sometimes randomly) in this allover design for a fashion fabric.'

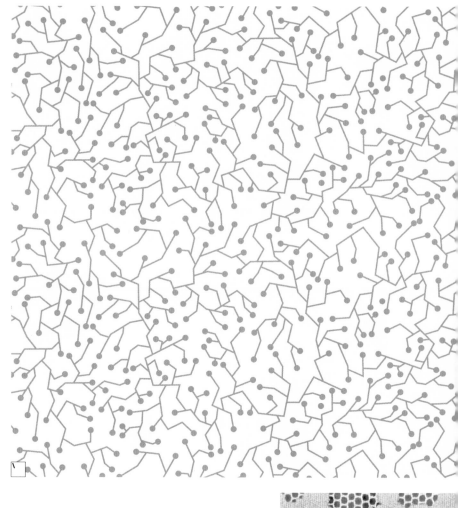

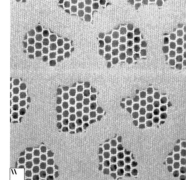

Abstract Patterns

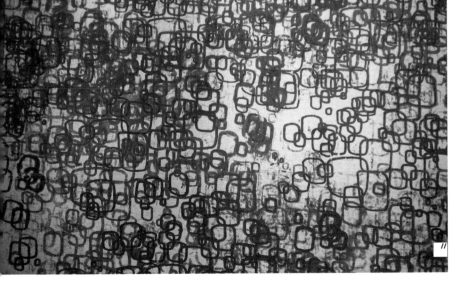

\ **Andrew Hardiman** for **Kuboaa** _ The artist remarks: 'A modern pattern designed to blend into a wall, so a pattern is only visible on nearer inspection. The original thought behind the design was to create something that was connected to each other but on a small pattern that would spread. This was loosely based on the "*Illuminati*", a secret organization with interconnecting strands.' \\ **Eugene Van Veldhoven** _ Tulle fabric with a hexagon shaped mesh effect forms the basis for this design. The artist comments: 'A graphic design has been etched on cotton with a burn out *(devoré)* chemical and laminated on to tulle.' **/ Dru Cole** _ Jewel-like brightly coloured triangles in this pattern have been created using dyes and masking fluid. **// Suse Schröder** _ Brown circles, like soap bubbles, float across a glowing background.

\

\\

Abstract Patterns

Els Van Baarle _ A background of multicolour dye has been brushed with freehand curving shapes in wax before being repainted, to create this ▯ric sample. \\ **Els Van Baarle** _ Shades of orange, merging into mauve and grey, underlie screenprinted symbols and letters in this complex ▯tern. It may have been inspired by the graffiti designs of urban artists who decorate tube trains and public places with their lively and irreverent ▯nments. **/ Els Van Baarle** _ Outlines of chairs can just about be made out in this multicoloured textile sample. **// Louise Kallinicou** _ Sinuous ▯apes based on pebbles and buildings are collaged over images of sea and skies. The artist comments: 'Photographic coastal imagery has been ▯laged and then intercut to produce a fluid form, reminiscent of wavelike motion.'

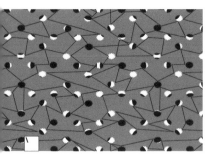

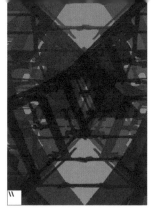

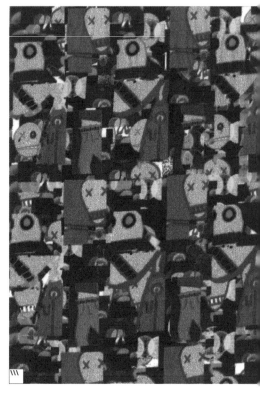

Abstract Patterns

Louise Gullick _ Black and white hemispheres joined together by thin black lines create this quirky design. The effect is one of effervescence as they vibrate against the brilliant scarlet background. **\\ Ed Jones** _ Red, yellow and purple hand screenprinted images form this textile sample. The many different colours are the result of overprinting with the screens. **\\\ Alex Edison** _ Multicoloured images of clothes and everyday items are used in this design. The artist comments: 'This graphic piece takes a lot of inspiration from modern illustrations, which generate a commentary on my life. I used CAD and screenprinting to create slight variations of image, which kept my personality in the piece.' **/ Petra Kather** _ A splash of scarlet over a grey and white patterned background makes up this pattern inspired by images of microbiology.

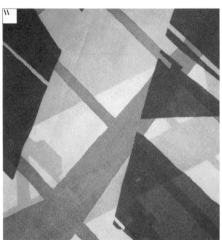

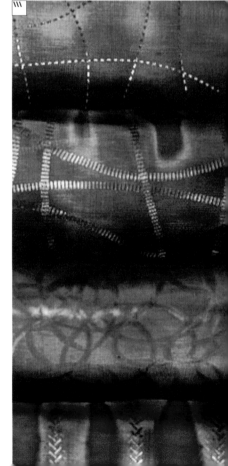

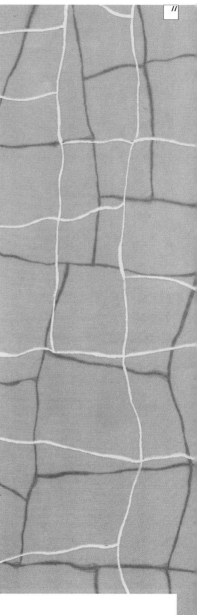

Els Van Baarle _ Vibrant sweeps of colour are juxtaposed with bold brushstrokes of black and interspersed white marks, which were made using hot wax as a resist. The overall effect is one of exuberance and excitement. **\\ Ed Jones** _ Simple overprinting with graphic shapes has been used to create this hand screenprinted textile design, inspired by the architectural form of Southampton Docks. **\\\ Janet Stoyel** for **ClothClinic.com** _ Coloured entirely by sound waves, the patterns on these pure metal woven materials have been produced without the use of dyes, chemicals or wet treatments of any kind. **/ Anna Ostrat** _ Two screenprinted blends in shades of mauve and orange – one on top of the other – produce this design of soft shapes floating on a base of graded or *ombré* colour. **// Cecilia Heffer** _ White and purple lines on an amethyst background feature in this simple but effective pattern, inspired by the idea of an aerial view of a cracked and hardened mud ground.

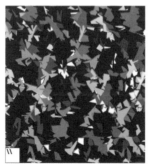

/

\ **Clare Perkins** _ Squiggles and curlicues have been printed and embroidered over a shocking pink background. This pink was the signature colour of the celebrated couturier Elsa Schiaparelli. \\ **Safa Maryam Taheri** _ The black background shows off to full effect this digital design of multicoloured figures fluttering in all directions. The artist comments: 'I was inspired by the work of Keith Haring when I created this pattern. I think his work is fantastic and this design adopts his striking sense of colour and boldness.' \\\ **Safa Maryam Taheri** _ Brilliant patches of fluorescent colour are combined in a digital design based on camouflage patterns. The artist comments: 'My inspiration was not nature but rather culture; making them unconventionally characterized as camouflage. I tend to work from geometric shapes and my colour palette usually combines black with flat, bold colour, which I suppose is influenced by graffiti.' **/ Els Van Baarle** _ Pink paper and black abstract shapes have been used in this textile sample, created using hot wax and dyes.

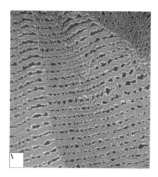

Abstract Patterns

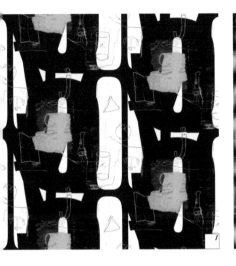

\ **Sally-Ann Murphy** _ This is an example of a *'shibori'* or resist dyed fabric produced in blue on a bright pink background. *Shibori* is the Japanese name for any process that dyes part of the cloth and deliberately prevents another part from being dyed. \\ **Alex Russell** _ Beige discs and magenta outlines feature in this design for fashion created with a layered series of patterns and drawings inspired by traditional textile imagery. / **Alex Russell** _ Faint chalk lines over a bold collage have created this fabric design, which combines a loose drawing style with clean graphic imagery. // **Darren Wilkinson Mawer** _ Knotted string was the inspiration for this tangled pattern of pink coloured squiggles set against a black and yellow background. It brings to mind the lights of Las Vegas, with its neon colours and diffused glow.

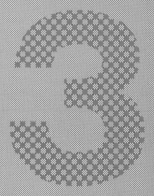

RETRO PATTERNS

'As is often the case in retro fashion, historical accuracy is somewhat beside the point.'

New York Times

Retro patterns are designs that are inspired by, or that seek to emulate, a previous era's style. They achieve this by using a combination of its characteristic colours and motifs[1] or by referencing illustrative styles of the period[2]. Designs that include icons of the period[3] naturally evoke the epoch, as do patterns that emulate art movements such as Op Art[4] or Pop Art[5] and designs that pay homage to an artist from a previous era[6]. Also included are designs that appear to capture the distinguishing mood of a period[7] or that use a retrospective style of colouring and technique[8].

[1] p.95 (right), p.101 (left)

[2] p.92, p.105 (left)

[3] p.102 (top right), p.106

[4] p.98 (top right), p.104

[5] p.113

[6] p.112 (top)

[7] p.100, p.107 (bottom)

[8] p.103, p.109 (top)

Dru Cole _ Entitled 'Parisols after Parisienne', this striking design references the ubiquitous black and white ceramics of the 1950s.

Dru Cole _ Looking like models from a 1950s *Vogue*, these elegant 'Blue Paris Ladies' parade with their dogs in this screenprinted silk sample.

Marc Burton _ White concentric circles form this deceptively simple pattern, which recalls the patterns of the Op Art movement of the 1960s, which explored visual effects resulting in illusions of three-dimensional form. **// Darren Wilkinson Mawer** _ Shades of blue have been used in this pattern formed of alternating 'ogee' shaped motifs, a sort of rounded diamond shape.

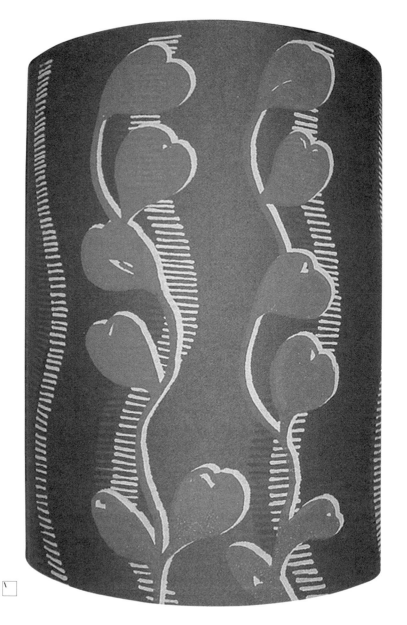

094

\ Charlotte Chamberlain _ This screenprinted lampshade in delicate shades of grey and blue has a design of undulating vertical stripes and plant forms, a frequently used combination of motifs in the 1950s. The artist comments: 'Inspired by London's contemporary architecture, this design mixes both natural foliage and geometric shapes.' **/ Rachel Cave** _ These curving lines and subtle colour palette recall the 'Scandinavian' look, which was fashionable in the 1950s. **// Rachel Cave** _ Expanding ovals of aqua produce a design that is reminiscent of the geometric patterns favoured in the early 1960s. Geometrics of all kinds were extremely popular as designers reflected the influences of contemporary fine artists and sculptors. **/// Darren Wilkinson Mawer** _ These collaged ellipses evoke the patterns of the 1970s, when designs such as these were widely used for wall coverings, lampshades and other interior design applications.

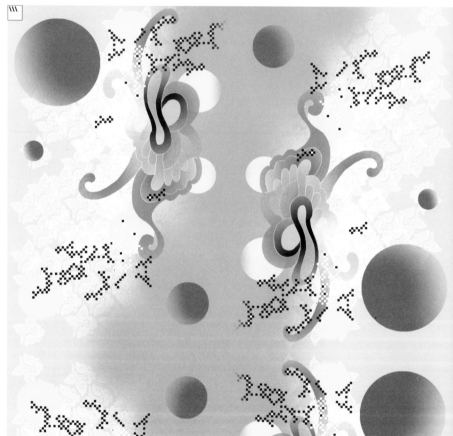

Caroline McNamara _ Silhouettes of fashion models in the characteristic dress and pose of the 1960s create a design for a fashion fabric. **James Pegg** _ Rectangles in powder blue are printed on to a black and white polka dot fabric, which calls to mind the favourite colourways of the 1950s. \\\ **Marie Hansen** _ The combination of the colours and cartoonlike motifs suggests the 1960s innovative animation film *The Yellow Submarine* which featured the music of the Beatles. / **Rachel Moore** _ Propeller like shapes are combined with strong verticals in this design, which draws inspiration from the Russian Constructivist movement of the 1920s and its celebration of machines.

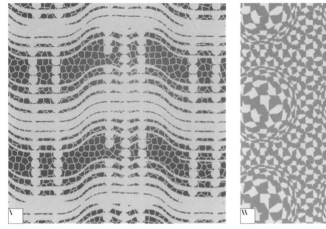

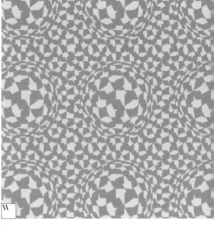

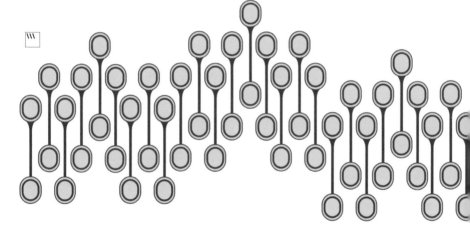

Yerin Jeon _ This wallpaper design resembles the nineteenth-century designs called 'eccentrics', which were stripes distorted into patterns that prefigured Op Art. The artist comments: 'These strong colours are easily noticed in a place like a bar or a club. Wavy, moving lines have been used to give the atmosphere of a combination of loud music and tipsy feelings.' **\\ Nathalie Pellon** _ Vibrating images play on the reaction of the human eye to colour and form in this design reminiscent of Op Art prints. **\\\ Ben Trill** for **Interim.org.uk** _ Green discs on vertical lines meander up and down in this pattern. The artist comments: 'The simplicity and flexibility of old designs, such as wallpaper from the 1960s, old bathroom tiles and parquet floors, inspired this design.' **/ Nadia Sparham** _ Wild and crazy funky flower shapes reach upwards in this design reminiscent of the Swinging Sixties.

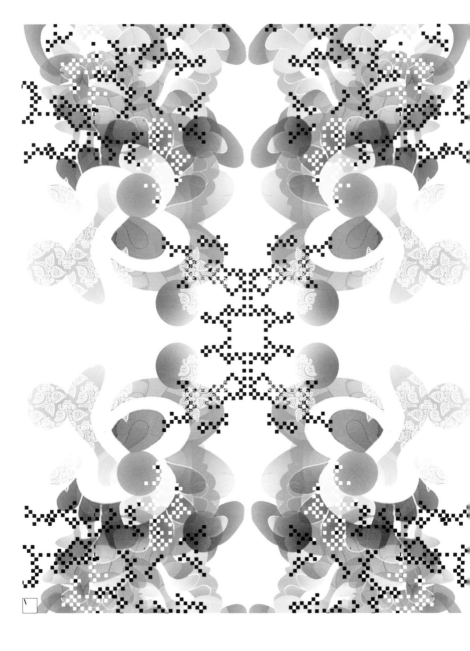

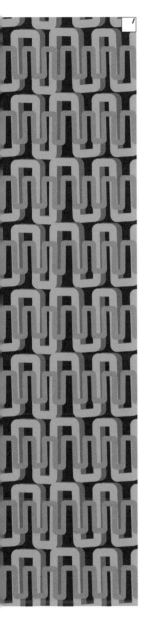

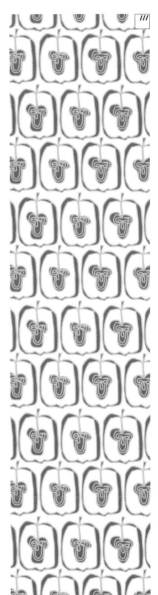

Marie Hansen _ A pastel coloured floral motif is overlaid with tiny black and white squares in this design, which evokes the psychedelic patterns of the 1960s. **/ Rachel Cave** _ Undulating lines have been shaded to give a three-dimensional appearance in this design for wallpaper. 3D effects were a very popular design device throughout the 1960s and early 1970s. **// Rachel Cave** _ Neat stylized flowers appear in this half-drop repeat for wallpaper in the 1960s signature colours of green, orange and brown. **/// Rachel Cave** _ Simple drawings of sections through apples have been put into a brick or masonry repeat in this wallpaper pattern.

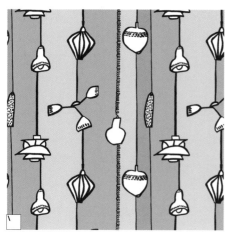

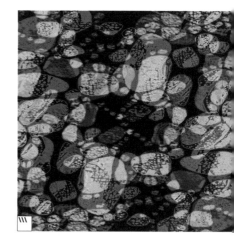

Nadia Sparham _ The outlines of lamps in this striped wallpaper have been inspired by several well-known designers of the time, including Poul Henningsen and Isamu Noguchi. **\\ Darren Wilkinson Mawer** _ Silhouettes of a young couple, sitting on invisible chairs, are featured in this screenprinted repeat, which recalls the credits for the TV programme *The Avengers*. This effect is heightened by the man's Beatle haircut and Cuban-heeled boots – both popular icons of the time. **\\\ Louise Killinicou** _ The artist comments: 'This pattern for wallpaper was inspired by 1950s patterns which used science and the abstractions of microscopic shapes. The manipulated texture appears in clusters of cell-like forms, reinforcing the molecular theme.' **/ Michelle Lucas** _ Clearly based on designs from the 1960s, this screenprinted wallpaper combines geometric patterns. The artist comments: 'I am intrigued by the reactions Op Art has on individuals, the deception through illusion which draws the viewer deeper into an image, creating the love for art.'

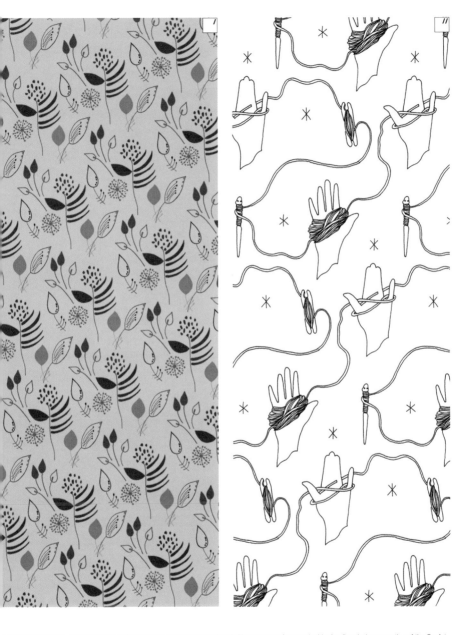

\ Dominic Meaker _ The grey outlines of this pattern converge to produce brilliant centres of orange in this dazzling design evocative of the Op Art movement of the 1960s. **/ Rachael Taylor** _ Delicately drawn leaves and flower heads evoke the characteristic graphic style of the celebrated 1950s designer, Lucienne Day. Day used her preferred media of the time – pen and ink – to produce a personal visual vocabulary of lines, dots and textures, which she used to create patterns for textiles and later for ceramics and plastic laminates. **// Nina Chakrabarti** _ A deceptively simple design of hands and yarn forms this pattern for the endpapers of Margaret Atwood's book *The Penelopiad*, which is a rewriting of Homer's *Odyssey*. The artist comments: 'I liked the idea of the infinite nature of the repeat pattern reflecting Penelope's constancy and patience. I was inspired by old annuals on knitting and weaving to produce a pattern that looked like a classic.'

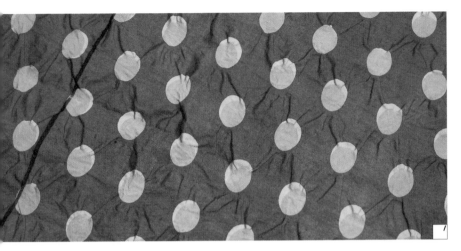

\ **Nadia Sparham** _ The sketched illustrations in this design are of iconic 1950s chairs and include the moulded rosewood and leather lounger and ottoman by American designer Charles Eames, which was first produced in 1956. **/ Ed Jones** _ This fabric sample, created using discharge and crimp paste, is one of the classic colour combinations for a polka dot – cream dots on a red background. Polka dots were hugely popular in the 1950s and featured on everything from dresses to decals. To discharge a dye means to remove it partially or completely. **// Karen Bravo** _ A vibrant image of a flower centre seems to explode on to the fabric in a burst of scarlet and pink. Slightly fuzzy or out of focus prints were prevalent in the 1960s and 1970s, reflecting the culture of the era.

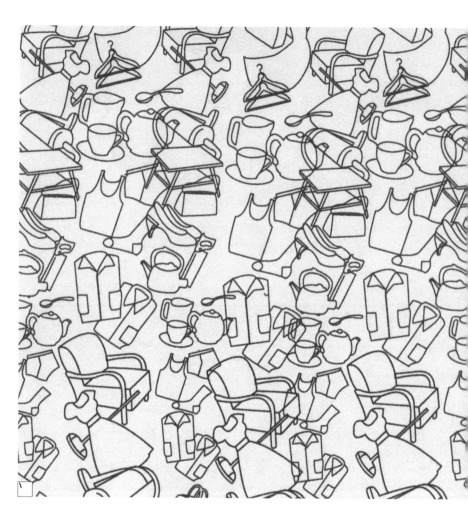

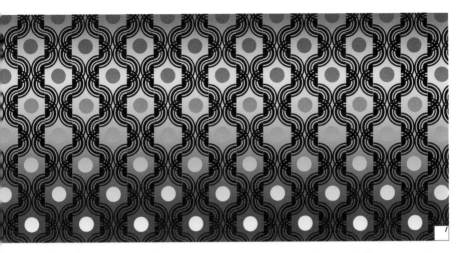

\ **Emily Alston** _ Everyday items have been drawn in fine red lines in this textile design. The items appear to date from the 1950s, for example, the cylinder vacuum cleaner and the classic electric kettle. **/ Marc Burton** _ Purple and mauve spots and a bold black motif have been printed on to an *ombré* copper coloured background in this wallpaper design, recalling the expensive metallic wall coverings of the 1970s. **// Darren Wilkinson Mawer** _ Floral silhouettes of male and female figures form a dynamic pattern on a black background. The blending of colours and images adds a typical 'flower power' quality to the design.

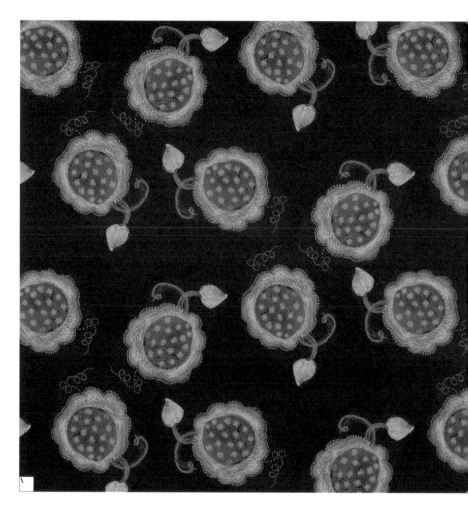

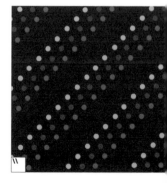

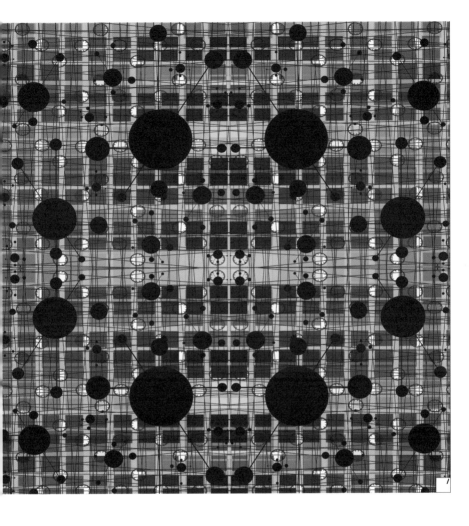

\ **Dru Cole**_Stylized flowers drawn in coloured pencil were digitally manipulated in this design for a fashion fabric. \\ **Darren Wilkinson Mawer** _
A simple pattern of diagonally repeated spots forms this design for men's ties. Dots of colour remain a firm favourite of designers and have never
been out of fashion. **/ Louise Gullick** _ Black discs of differing sizes give a three-dimensional quality to this intricate design.

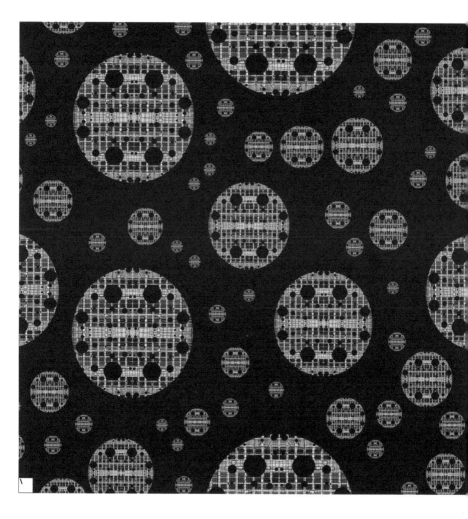

Retro Patterns

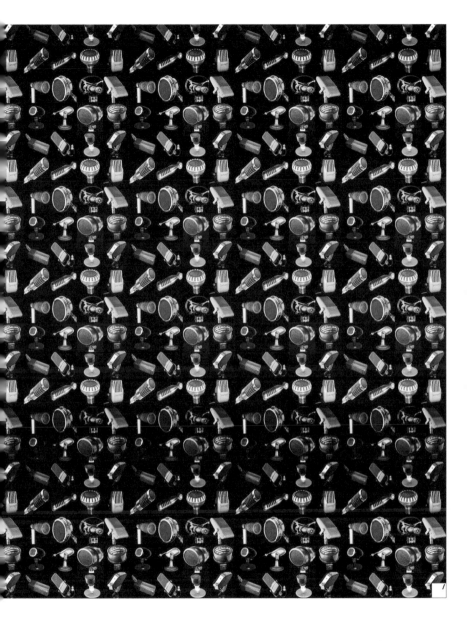

Louise Gullick _ Paying homage to the work of Op Art painter Victor Vasarely, this design shares the characteristic feeling of movement and three-dimensional forms typical of the artist's work. **\\ Rachel Cave** _ Bold teardrop shapes use mirror imaging on a vertical axis in this digital design reminiscent of 1960s wallpapers. **/ Peggy Cole** _ Vintage microphones have been chosen as motifs in this design, which echoes the rhythm and repetition seen in the work of Pop artists such as Andy Warhol.

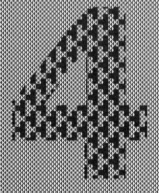

GEOMETRIC PATTERNS

'Pattern is both uplifting and calming to live with. It reflects the repetition found in nature and creates inspiring spaces.'

Dominic Crinson

Geometric patterns are nonrepresentational patterns that have been arranged into an ordered or regular repeat. Some of these designs have an entirely mathematical basis[1] and almost all have an underlying invisible geometric grid upon which the pattern is constructed[2]. Several of the designs have a regular structure, which the artists then deliberately interrupt[3] to achieve an asymmetrical balance to their patterns. A few of the artists do not use a formal arrangement at all for their designs[4], but still manage to attain a geometric look. Digital techniques are particularly successful in constructing regular patterns[5], which are then digitally printed[6] or screenprinted[7]. Texture serves to soften the rigid outlines of geometric designs, especially when a soft fabric such as felt is manipulated into a design[8] or when plastics are incorporated into a weave[9].

[1] p.118, p.121 (top)

[2] p.124

[3] p.120 (bottom), p.137 (right)

[4] p.122, p.143 (left)

[5] p.126 (bottom), p.145

[6] p.126 (top)

[7] p.155 (top)

[8] p.147

[9] p.172 (top)

\ Ben Trill for **Interim.org.uk** _ Octagonal interlocking shapes give this pattern a feeling of movement and vitality. The artist comments: 'My work is influenced by science and often feels very organic and playful. I took the bar element from our own logo and let it grow in a self-evolving image.' **\\ Ben Trill** for **Interim.org.uk** _ Squares, rectangles and diagonal lines compose this pattern. The artist comments: 'We are always interested in loops and symmetry. The influence for this design was Aztec carvings and drawings, revisited using a fresh graphical approach.' **\\\ Nathalie Pellon** _ Entitled 'Talisman', this precisely constructed pattern is composed of intersecting arcs and was inspired by the Celtic symbol for the solar system. **/ Petra Kather** _ Printmaking techniques may have been the source of the understated marks used in this pattern, as they appear to have been incised rather than drawn or painted.

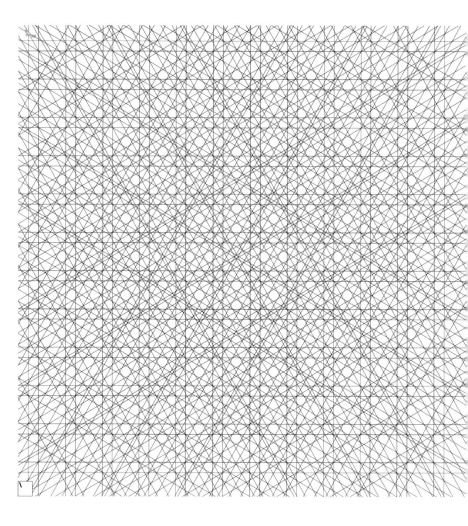

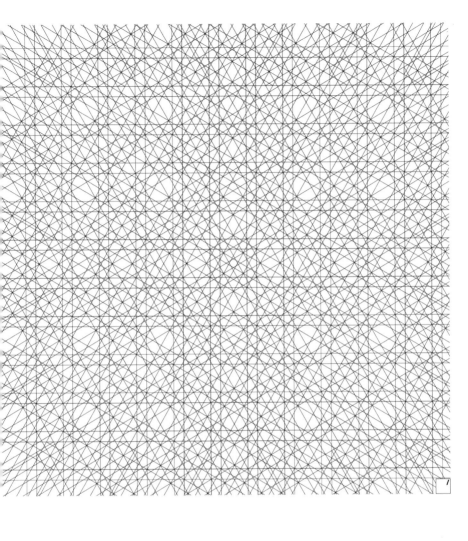

\ **Stefan Hanser** _ The artist states: 'I work out non-expressive, concrete systematic designs and patterns by using mathematically based methods, signs and graphical elements, which are set into relation to a graphical pattern, to create reduced aesthetic information that can be perceived by the viewer by active analysis.' \\ **Bathsheba Grossman** for **Materialise.MGX** _ Selective Laser Sintering (SLS) was the technique responsible for this truly amazing lighting device entitled 'Quintrino' with its interconnecting spirals that twist in and around each other like mating starfish. The artist comments: 'This design marks the end of a series that has spanned my sculptural life to date, progressing through the five Platonic solids to the last and most mystical of all, the twelve-sided dodecahedron. In this fifth shape Plato saw the nature and wholeness of the entire universe, the spiritual quintessence. This light structure is a household embodiment of that unity: the Quintrino.' **/ Stefan Hanser** _ This pattern is part of a series of graphic patterns entitled 'Interference'.

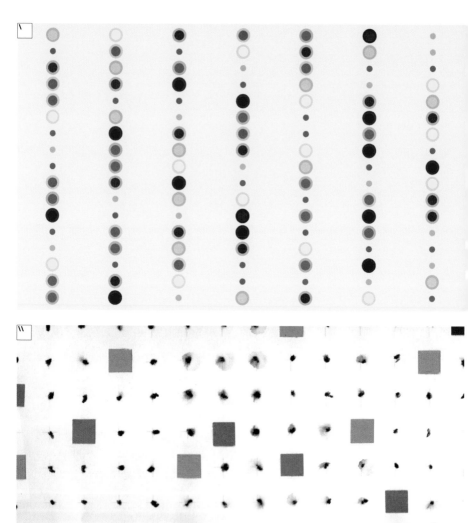

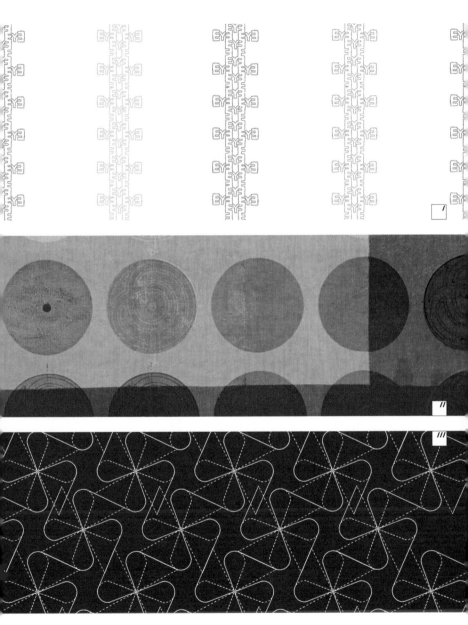

Marina Strumphler _ Neatly arranged, vertical lines of multicoloured spots and concentric circles form this digitally produced design. The colour and tension between the forms is an important feature in this apparently simple design. **\\ Marina Strumphler** _ Cut squares of coloured paper have been collaged with spots of black ink to create this fabric design. With its spare colour scheme and minimalist style, it may have been influenced by the paintings of Piet Mondrian. **/ Gavin Wilshen** _ Entitled 'i-pattern', these understated vertical stripes are composed entirely of the letters E and Y. **// Joanna Kinnersley-Taylor** _ Inscribed discs in shades of indigo blue appear in a grid arrangement in this hand-dyed and printed textile. It is one of three works sited in the Mater Hospital, Belfast, Northern Ireland, UK. **/// Joanna Kinnersley-Taylor** _ This discharge printed textile has been hand dyed using indigo and forms part of a design for aprons and Wellington boots for workers on Fish Quay, North Shields, Tyne and Wear, UK.

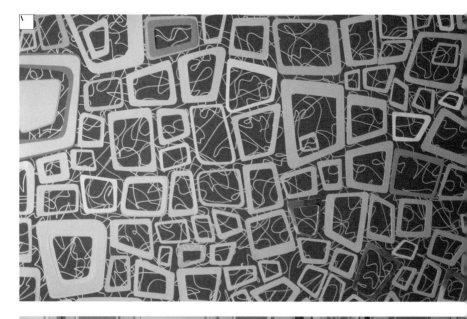

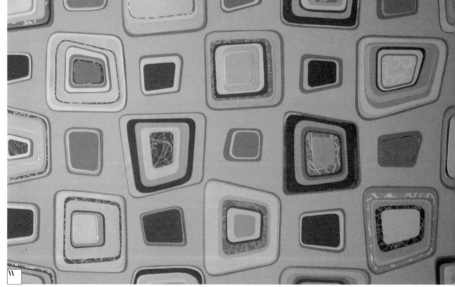

Geometric Patterns

Naomi Bolt _ Collages of rounded geometric forms in shades of blue and mauve form this series of designs intended for gift wrap and paper products. **\\ Naomi Bolt** _ Blue geometric shapes on mauve were inspired by a visit to Barcelona. The artist states: 'The intention was to capture the strikingly eye-catching reaction that both Joan Miró and Antonio Gaudí evoke in their various works by using a vibrant, bold and contemporary colour palette.' **/ Naomi Bolt** _ A detail from the series based on Barcelona; the artist comments: 'A mixed media approach, working with various materials, to contrast the matt and shiny qualities with the adding and taking away of the surface, to subtly transform the designs from two-dimensional to three-dimensional.'

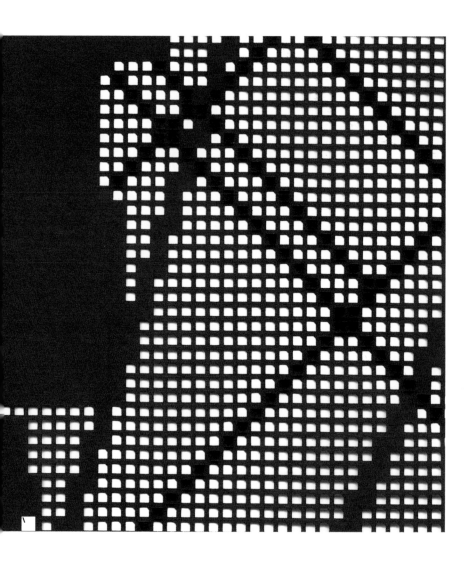

124

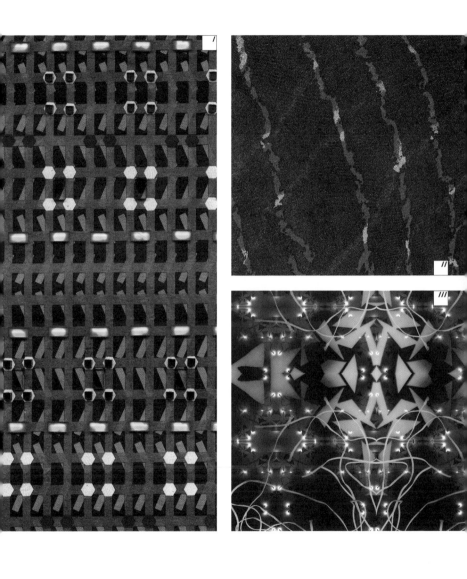

Sarah Angold _ Squares of white and black on cobalt give a dynamic geometric impression of Brighton's ruined pier collapsing into the brilliant blue winter sea. **/ Sarah Angold** _ The artist comments: 'Four layers of laser cut and bonded fabrics form an elaborate and opulent repeat that subtly evolves down its length.' **// Sara Sulemanji** _ Diamond shapes are produced by the overprinting of lines in this pattern, while the brush strokes add texture. It was inspired by the markings on tropical fish. **/// Maria Yaschuk** _ Light emitting diodes (LEDs) have been included in this wall hanging and emanate light – albeit very subtly. The artist comments: 'The world around us is a beautiful and fascinating pattern of chaos and ordered complexity. I am captivated by its mysterious structure and the way we create and incorporate our structures within it. 'Wire Geometrics' is the collection that explores the connection and interdependence of real physical space and the virtual space created by the surrounding environment.'

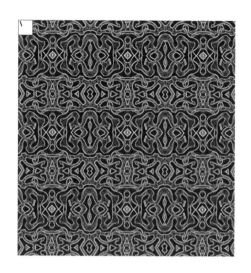

Caroline McNamara _ Reminiscent of a Persian carpet in its complexity, this dazzling pattern echoes the arabesques and intertwining tendrils so beloved of classic Islamic designs. In fact, it draws inspiration from Gaudí's magnificent buildings in Barcelona. **\\ Dominic Crinson** _ Moorish tile designs and colours are the inspiration for this dense, multicoloured pattern. This particular design has been produced as a ceramic tile for walls or floors and uses muted tones to enhance its symmetry. **/ Dominic Crinson** _ Tile designs based on mathematical principles were the starting point for this design. The artist comments: 'My speciality is designing imagery to be output via computer on to various surfaces such as ceramic tiles, wallpaper, carpet and floor tiles.'

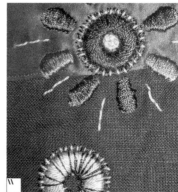

Geometric Patterns

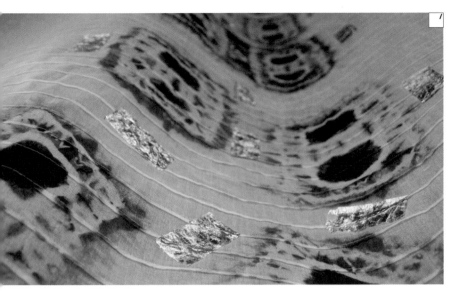

Eugene Van Veldhoven _ Elongated and textured blue squares in this pattern suggest the designs of the Art Deco period. The artist remarks: 'This design has been produced by printing on to a polyamide fabric with an expanding PVC ink. The print is an enlargement of a weaving structure.' Donna Bailey _ Hand embroidery embellishes silk and linen in this sample inspired by cogs and wheels. **/ Vivien Prideaux** _ Wavelike patterns re formed by using 'shibori' or resist techniques on to cotton organza, before adding tiny squares of gold leaf. The artist comments: 'Inspired by e way the light plays its magic at a given moment, the unifying thread through my work continues to be based on informed perception of the awe-spiring beauty of my native Cornish seascape.' **// Vivien Prideaux** _ Hand dyed with indigo dye and gold leaf on hemp fabric. The artist remarks: 'his piece is part of an ongoing series entitled 'Tied Lines – Tide Lines' that explores the inspirational images made by the interaction of water, nd, waves and sky.'

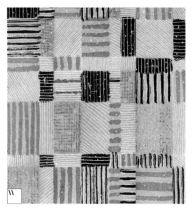

Sandra Setyawan _ Snowflakes and Christmas decorations are combined in this pattern for seasonal gift wrap. **\\ Dru Cole** _ A simple grid pattern forms the basis for this hand-painted design. It was scanned and digitally manipulated to give this colourway. **\\\ Sandra Setyawan** _ The inspiration for this pattern was the Alpine region of Switzerland and its flora and fauna. The flowers are stylized versions of the blue gentians that flourish there. **/ Lena Corwin** _ Flattened flowers and leaves float across a background of jagged blue and white diamonds in this fabric sample. The angular silhouettes form a vibrant contrast to the organic shapes.

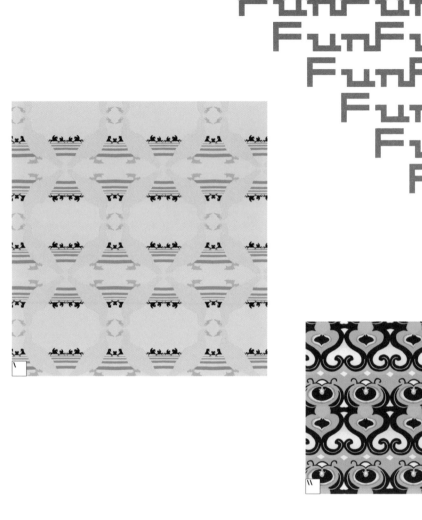

Vicky Graham _ Part of the 'Mary Poppins Dissected' series. The artist comments: 'This is a silhouette of a duck with a simple stripe of a statue of a horse sitting upon a zebra crossing. A line drawing of the duck was positioned off centre and the whole piece put into repeat.' **\\ Rachel Moore** _ Rounded edge forms echo and exaggerate the heart-shaped figure that lies at the core of each motif in this screenprinted textile design. **Delaware** _ The word 'Fun' repeated over and over again makes up this simple but effective pattern. The designer lists her influences as including: Japanese kimono, towel and haiku, Andy Warhol, Shotaro Ikenami (Japanese novelist), Minimal Art, David Bowie, Roy Lichtenstein, Moo! (Japanese TV drama), tea ceremony...'

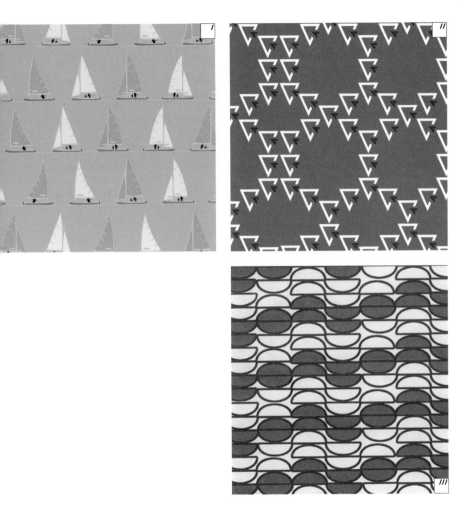

\ James Pegg _ Based on a building façade, this digitally printed silk becomes an alternative to a woven plaid fabric. The artist says about his work: 'By using modern equipment I was able to bring a painterly quality to my patterns, maintaining individual brushstrokes through the use of digital printing, while using screenprinting to keep sharpness to my handdrawn lines.' **/ Emily Burningham** _ Neat rows of small yachts glide across a calm aqua background in this design. The alternating shapes of the sails make the pattern appear to undulate and move ever so slightly, almost as if the boats were becalmed. **// Saviane Auzende** for **Mekanism** _ White triangles are arranged in a hexagonal repeat for this pattern for skateboards. **/// Yerin Jeon** _ The artist comments: 'This pattern is developed from the images of minerals. I have used white for the background to emphasize the beauty of the space, which is the most important characteristic feature of Korean traditional paintings.'

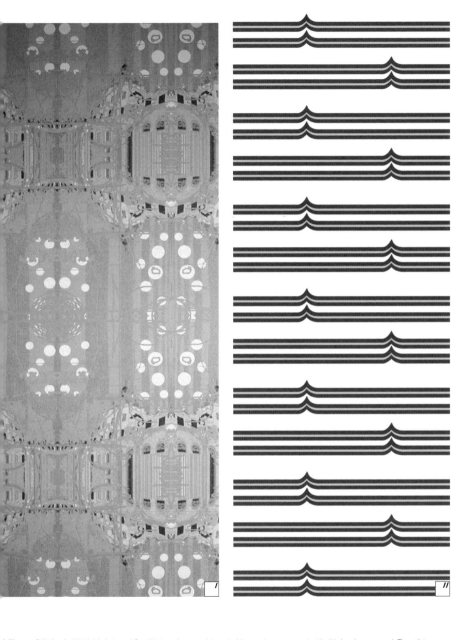

\ Eleanor Pritchard _ Welsh blankets and Scottish tweeds were reinterpreted in a contemporary context in this handwoven panel. The artist comments: 'The colours are inspired by the familiar nostalgic palette of mid-twentieth century English art – painters such as Ben Nicholson and Eric Ravillious – with their combination of soft chalky tones and bright accents.' **/ Vicky Graham** _ Multicoloured stripes and outlines of buildings form this intriguing design, from the 'Mary Poppins Dissected' series. The artist remarks: 'This was originally a drawing of roof tops in London with polka dots in the background. A detail of the building was picked out, the colour palette changed and the whole design put into repeat.' **// Ben Trill** for **Interim.org.uk** _ Horizontal stripes with a blip in them make this pattern look somewhat like a seismograph. The artist comments: 'The use of negative space in this design is what makes it most interesting. It's almost a design within a design.'

THE WORLD IS FULL OF FASCINATING PROBLEMS WAITING TO BE SOLVED.

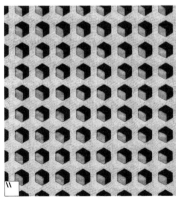

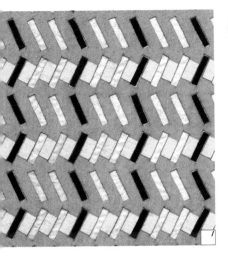

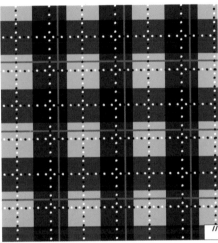

\ **Delaware** _ 'The World is Full of Fascinating Problems Waiting to be Solved' is the title of this design. How true! The elements of this pattern recall those of cross stitch – a form of embroidery once seen as old-fashioned, but now experiencing a comeback as part of the general craft revival. \\ **Sarah Angold** _ Three-dimensional boxes in shades of indigo blue appear to float in rectilinear formation across a yellow background. The artist comments: 'The bright seaside colours accentuate the simple playfulness of this pattern, which was created by staggering three layers of laser-cut fabrics.' **/ Sarah Angold** _ Rectangles have been arranged to form an eye-dazzling pattern. The artist remarks: 'This was inspired by the evening sunlight reflecting off the sea, combined with the shadows cast by Brighton's turquoise beach railings.' **// Darren Wilkinson Mawer** _ This pattern with its striking colourway might be seen as a contemporary tartan, with its green and mauve stripes giving a curious combination of colours. The lines of black and white dots serve to confuse the eye and aesthetic sensibilities even further.

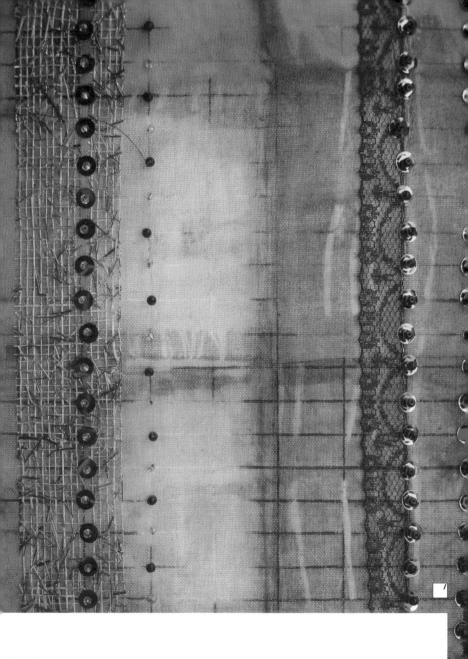

Nathalie Pellon _ Interlocking arcs in green over discs of yellow and mauve form this regular repeating pattern. **\\ Joanna Kinnersley-Taylor** _ Swirls in white on yellow ochre and blue have been screenprinted on to wool for this piece entitled 'Balcony Skirts'. It has been externally sited for the Fisherman's Mission on Fish Quay, North Shields, Tyne and Wear, UK. **/ Keira March** _ Canvas has been painted and dyed using a variety of techniques. The artist elaborates: 'Indigo and black dye has been used to render the surface texture slightly random. Once completed I additionally worked into the surface by sewing strips of lace and sequins on it.'

Geometric Patterns

Delaware _ The geometric figures in this pattern, which resemble stylized Oriental ideograms, also have a similarity to the Pac-Man pop culture icon of the 1980s. **\\ Saviane Auzende** for **Mekanism** _ Triangles of yellow ochre enlivened by bright blue, looking somewhat like tiny tents in a desert, make up this design for skateboards. **/ Eugene Van Veldhoven** _ Golden yellow flocked fibres create the raised texture on this fabric sample. The image was inspired by the microscopic images of penicillin. **// James Pegg** _ Brown circles on an orange background feature in this screenprinted textile sample. The hand drawn quality comes from using a wax crayon in the original illustration.

Geometric Patterns

Sandra Setyawan _ Chamois deer from the Alpine region of Switzerland, together with squares of rust and olive green, form this geometric pattern for paper products. **/ Delaware** _ Multicoloured squares form the basis for this pattern, which features the image of a dog barking at the sun. The shaded effect of each square makes the design look rather like an openwork fabric of the type used for cross-stitch embroidery. Cross stitch is cited as one of the designer's inspirations, together with John Whitney (early computer graphics designer), Jamie Reed, Michelangelo Antonioni (movie director), Beatles, Flying Lizards (band), Old School/Hip Hop, Dub Sound and John McEnroe (tennis player).

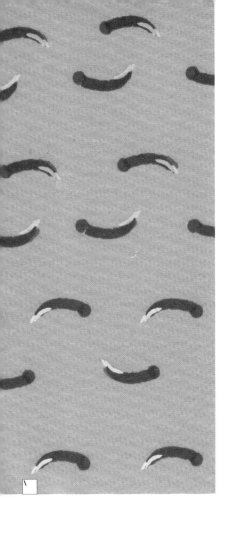

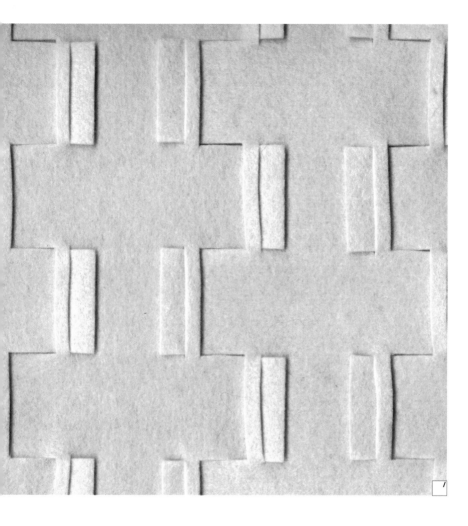

Denise Boyle _ Squiggles and dots sweep across this design in a precise and orderly manner. They may have been inspired by the movements of synchronized swimmers or perhaps by discarded matches? Smoking and its associated paraphernalia were popular motifs for early photomontages. **Nathalie Pellon** _ Long-barrelled guns are arranged into a diamond shaped repeat for wall coverings. In decorative design, weapons have traditionally been used to symbolize the triumph of good over evil. **/ Marina Strumphler** _ Felt rectangles have been cut and manipulated to create geometric pattern.

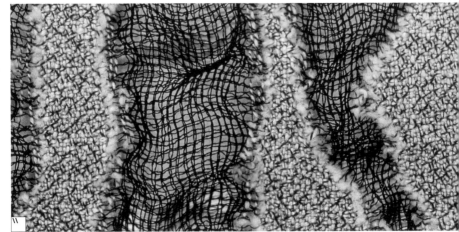

/

\ Maria Yaschuk _ LEDs twist like meandering snakes across this wall hanging, adding an oddly organic feeling to the pattern. The artist states: 'Through playing with light patterns and integrating lighting technologies into wallpaper, I am trying to construct a powerful, majestic and futuristic atmosphere in the interior.' **\\ Eugene Van Veldhoven** _ Vertical bands of different weaves and weights of fabric appear to have been combined in this sample. On closer inspection, it is evident that the open weave is a result of a textile treatment known as *devoré* or 'burn out'. **/ James Pegg** _ Digitally printed on to silk chiffon, this print nonetheless has a handpainted look. The artist comments: 'The silk was used so that the geometry of the print became softer and a masculine print becomes suitable for women's wear.'

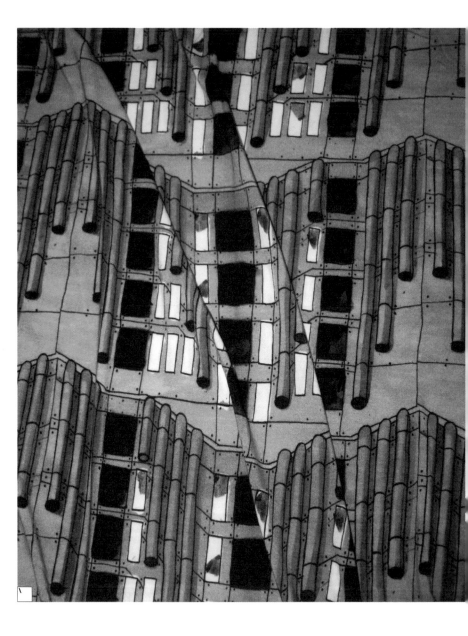

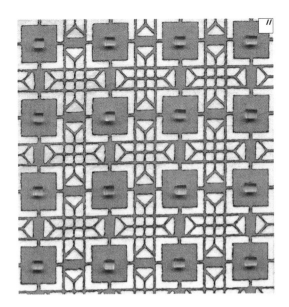

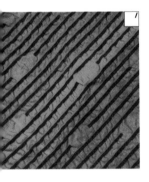

James Pegg _ Using windows as inspiration, this viscose jersey was digitally printed in muted pink and black. The artist remarks: 'The print was designed with sweeping horizontal lines so the jersey could be draped to form a contrast between the soft lines of the fabric and the harsh geometric line drawings.' **/ Ed Jones** _ Cotton has been dyed red then black and discharge and crimp paste applied to create continuous folds and tucks on this fabric sample. **// Sarah Angold** _ These complex red shapes were inspired by the tiny panes of glass in old-fashioned lead windows. **/// Andrew Hardiman** for **Kuboaa** _ Burgundy on red in an angular arrangement makes up this imposing pattern for a large format wall covering.

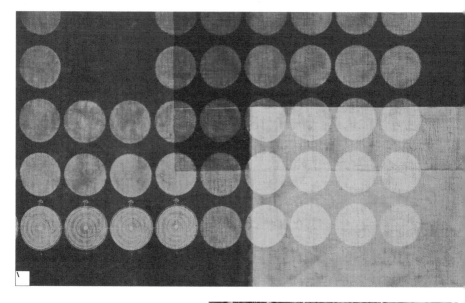

Joanna Kinnersley-Taylor _ Inscribed discs have been discharge printed over maroon rectangular shapes in this pattern, which is part of a series of works sited in the Mater Hospital, Belfast, Northern Ireland, UK. **\\ Dominic Crimson** _ These intense kaleidoscopic images for ceramic tiles are from a series entitled 'Glitz'. The artist comments: 'I have always used a lot of colour and patterning in my designs, enabling me to create dramatic, eye-catching interiors. The designs come from photographic sources, which are input directly into a computer via a scanner or camera, and manipulated to form enlarged organic matter and repeat pattern forms.' **/ Nathalie Pellon** _ 'Spirograph' patterns have evidently been the basis for this web of interlocking arcs. **// Victoria Graham** _ Renaissance architecture has been digitally manipulated to form this pattern for wallpaper.

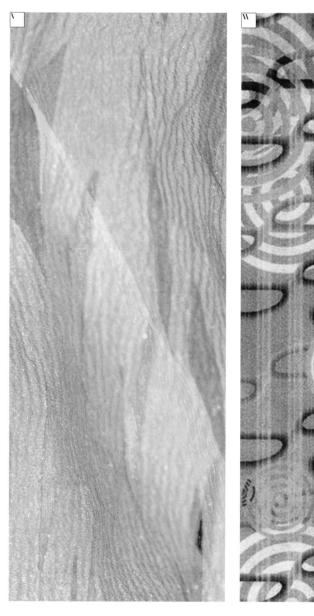

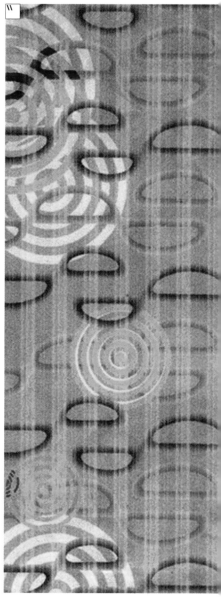

Geometric Patterns

Eugene Van Veldhoven _ Wavelike shapes of pale pink, magenta and yellow have been produced in this fabric sample. The artist elaborates: 'Two different coloured layers of crepe voile have been slit by a laser, creating many different mixtures of the two colours.' **\\ Yerin Jeon** _ Concentric circles and hemispheres feature in this computer-generated pattern. The artist remarks: 'Based on pebbles, the circles in this pattern represent the ages of the lines that had been made by pressure and time.' **/ Rachel Moore** _ Grey, yellow and two tones of pink have been combined to produce a pattern of three-dimensional boxes in this hand screenprinted textile. **// Dominic Crinson** _ A single digitally produced tile with sparkling highlights. The artist observes: 'Pattern is both uplifting and calming to live with. It reflects the repetition found in nature and creates inspiring spaces.'

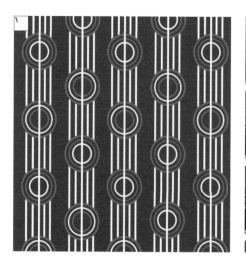

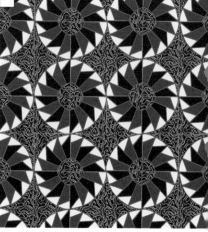

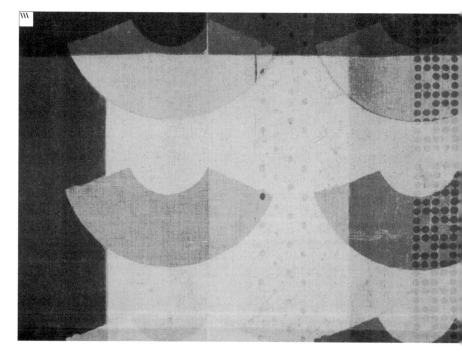

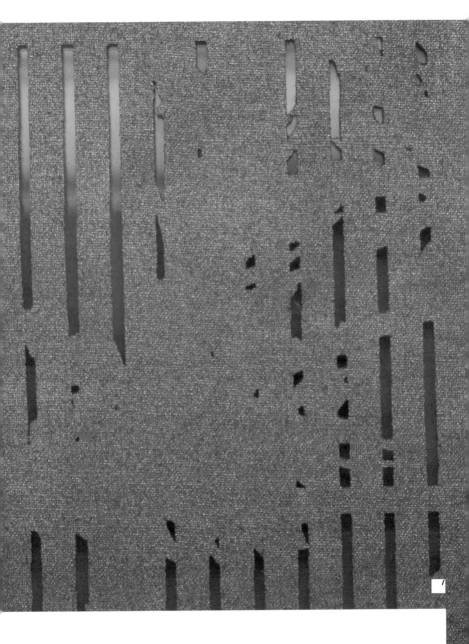

Marc Burton _ The regular concentric circles and straight white lines of this repeat have been drawn with military precision in this design for wallpaper. \\ **Caroline McNamara** _ Spinning wheel shapes are repeated over a background of multicolour tracery in this digital textile design. \\ **Joanna Kinnersley-Taylor** _ Dots, rectangles and collar shapes feature in this textile, which has been created by hand dyeing and discharge printing methods. To discharge a dye means to remove it partially or completely. / **Eugene Van Veldhoven** _ Thin strips of purple fabric have been removed using a 'burn out' or *devoré* chemical to produce a graphic design. *Devoré* is a popular technique with textile designers, not least because of its inherent element of unpredictability.

Geometric Patterns

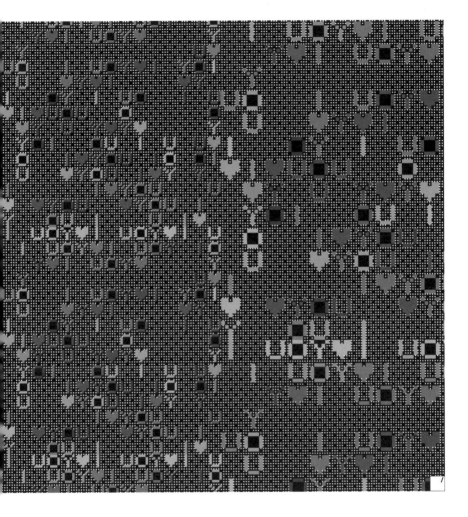

Veronica Pock _ This wall covering is part of a collection of designs entitled 'A Twist of Fate?'. The artist explains: 'This series explores the idea of chaos theory, which reveals itself in ever-repeating patterns taking place on differing scales and from different perspectives. This design zooms in to pixel level and was made using screenprinting, jacquard weaving and digital printing techniques.' **/ Delaware** _ 'I love you' is the sentiment spelt out in this digital design. The letters are repeated over and over again, using different colours and sizes of type in such a way as to resemble hand embroidery, which holds a fascination for this artist.

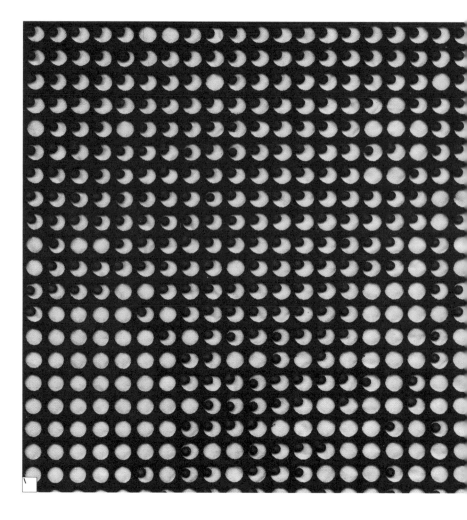

160 Geometric Patterns

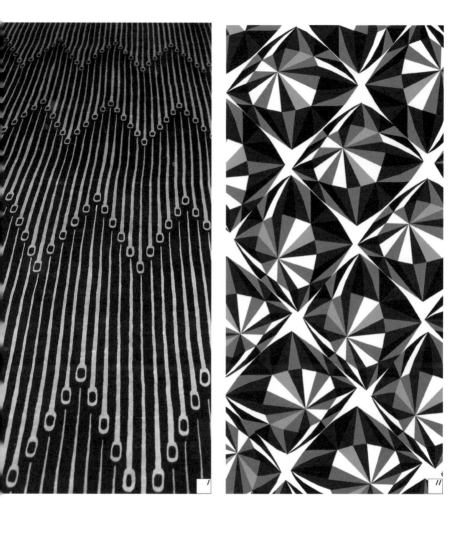

Sarah Angold _ Discs of fabric have been cut out and replaced by irregularly placed dots in this eye-dazzling design. The artist comments: 'This is a subtle twist on a straightforward repeat pattern, inspired by clusters of mussels on Brighton beach.' **/ Emily Anderson** _ Grossly enlarged sewing needles have been used to make a striking zig-zag pattern in this hand screenprinted textile. **// Nathalie Pellon** _ Shards of black, white and grey create this design, which has the disquieting effect of appearing to be three-dimensional. It is based on the shapes of diamonds 'in the rough', that before being cut and polished.

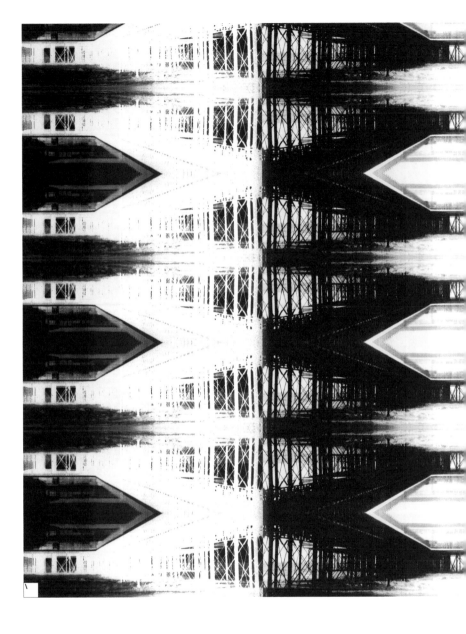

162

ah Devey _ A seaside pier was the unlikely source of this striking digital design. The artist comments: 'This image was inspired by a dark, rainy t Weston-super-Mare, where I had a caravan holiday.' **/ Sarah Devey** _ Bold black and white stripes are relieved by naturalistically drawn r heads in a design for gift wrap and paper products.

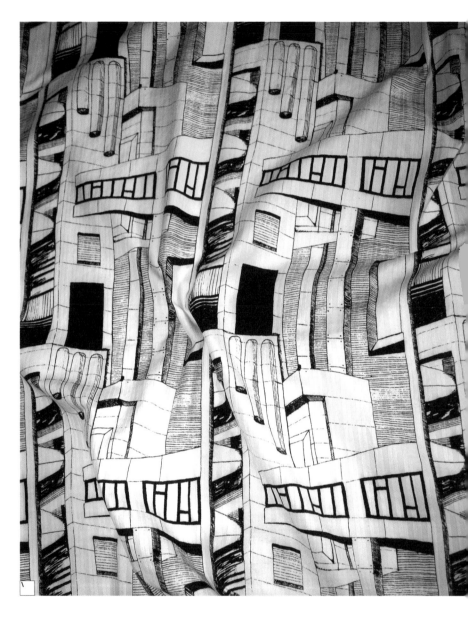

James Pegg _ Inspired by the architecture of Leeds and Berlin, this sample of hand screenprinted fabric makes a statement about the contrast between the decay of the old against the regeneration of the new. **/ James Pegg** _ A hand drawn repeat for a textile based on Nottingham Trent University. The artist comments: 'I looked at buildings most people would not give a second glance to, but I created a collection that made them aesthetically change.'

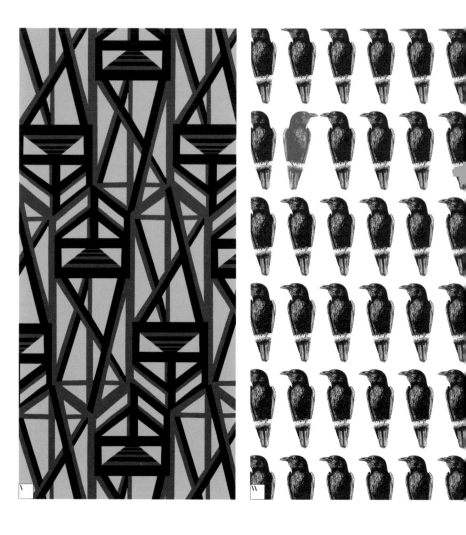

Geometric Patterns

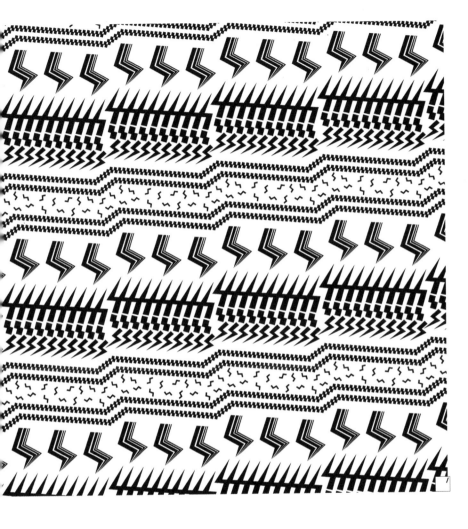

\ **Rachel Moore** _ Entitled 'Pylons', this screenprinted textile uses interplay of angular lines in two shades of grey. It clearly suggests the rigidity of the structure it replicates, as well as producing a dynamic design. \\ **Sarah Devey** _ This design of black birds all in a row, except one blue one, recalls a favourite childhood book, *The Blue Bird* by Moris Meterlink, which was about a magical bird that brings happiness. / **Giovanna Cellini** _ Black and white repeated 'S' shapes in this design provide an example of the way that the eye interprets counterchange between dark on light and light on dark as vibrant movement.

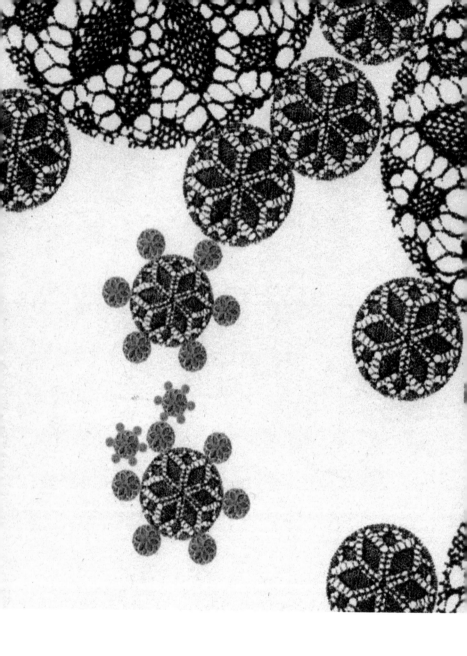

Geometric Patterns

Emily Alston _ Circles of lace, resembling snowflakes, have been arranged into a pattern for a large format wall covering. Each lace circle is identical, unlike snowflakes, which grow in a fractal manner and are never exactly alike.

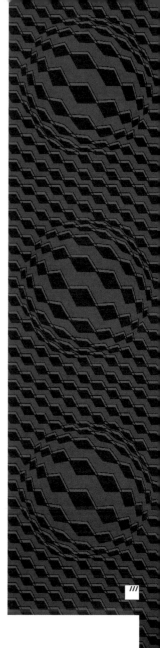

Jiri Evenhuis for **Materialise.MGX** _ Reminiscent of a futuristic city floating in space, this extraordinary construction entitled 'Metropolis' is a ghting device made from polyamide by the Selective Laser Sintering (SLS) technique. **/ Heather Power** _ Horizontal lines of repeating symbols fill he available space, resulting in a satisfying balance between the black and white marks employed. **// Heather Power** _ A densely packed, grid-ased pattern resembling Nigerian 'adire' or resist-dyed fabrics. **/// Natalie Pellon** _ Vivid optical effects are created in this digitally produced esign for a textile, in which a mass of diamond shapes seems to shift before our eyes.

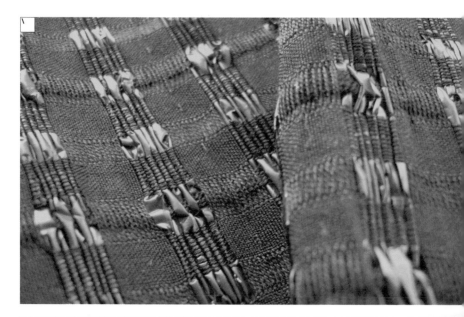

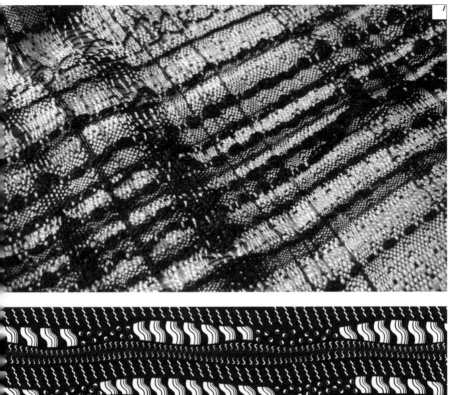

Keira March _ Twisted bin bags have been used to make part of the weft in this unusual handwoven fabric inspired by Gothicism. **\\ Keira March** _ An open weave in black and violet hand-dyed yarns make up this sample. The artist comments: 'I developed this piece from an idea of a spider's web, but also into research into Gothicism – which is where the inspiration of the colour palette came from. The violet is supposed to represent the more spiritual ideas of death and the black the unknown.' **/ Keira March** _ The textures in this woven textile have been created by a method of cramming and spacing the yarns, so the weft becomes more prominent in some areas compared to others. **// Giovanna Cellini** _ This eye-dazzling design is made up of undulating zig-zags of white 'S' shapes on black, which create a visually disturbing pattern.

ORGANIC PATTERNS

'A fabric design concretely captures the moment through the skill of the artist, who responds unconsciously to the place and time in which he lives.'

Mariano Fortuny

Organic patterns portray the natural forms of flora and fauna and fall into what is considered to be the most popular of the design categories. Observational drawing plays a major part in the creation of these designs[1], often with an emphasis on the realistic depiction of fruit, flowers, leaves[2] and animals[3]. Many designers stylize their portrayal of plants[4] to achieve their aims. Several of the patterns depicted are influenced by Japanese art[5], or by scenes inspired by Scandinavian[6] or English landscapes[7]. This category of patterns relies profoundly on the juxtaposition of the colours used and these can be very intense[8], or subtle[9], or dramatic[10] or restrained[11], while still being accessible and agreeable.

[1] p.190, p.237 (bottom right),

[2] p.177, p.186 (top), p.220 (top)

[3] p.201, p.216 (right)

[4] p.195 (bottom centre), p.234 (bottom right)

[5] p.194

[6] p.227

[7] p.192 (top)

[8] p.228 (top)

[9] p.187 (bottom)

[10] p.220 (bottom left), p.233

[11] p.237 (bottom right)

176

James Pegg _ An unusual assortment of creatures has been included in this black and white design of collaged photographic images. The artist explains: 'This design was a parody of old fabrics where instead of using conventional "pretty" animals I used vultures, camels, hippos and bears.' **Joanna Basford _** This detail from 'Crazy Botanic' shows the wealth of meticulous drawing that has been used to create this pattern. **/ Joanna Basford _** Tiny drawings arranged into a circular form are joined by trailing tendrils. One side of the motif is denser than the other giving a three-dimensional quality to the design. The artist writes: 'From afar "Crazy Botanic" appears as a ball of sprawling flora and vines; closer inspection reveals delicate drawings of imagined blossoms and vines, teeming with curious beasties and butterflies.'

178 Organic Patterns

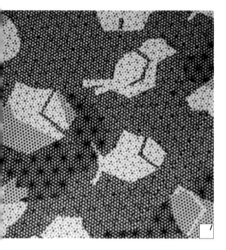

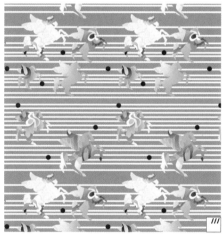

Giovanna Cellini _ Heart-shaped leaves and berries are drawn in opposing cross-hatched lines to produce this screenprint. The artist comments: 'Although this design was put together digitally, the lines are hand drawn and give a certain movement to the overall effect.' **/ Marloes Jongen** _ Dots have been overlaid to compose this dense pattern of stylized fishes and sea creatures. There is a feeling of revolution in the design as the tiny, repeated spots take on a pattern of their own. **// Marloes Jongen** _ Vertical lines staggered at intervals create this curious pattern of fish. More dashes and a birdlike creatures have been drawn on top with a red pen, adding to the unusual nature of the design. **/// Marie Hansen** _ Fantastic flying horses made of multicoloured patterns are set against lines and dots resembling musical notation, in this digital design.

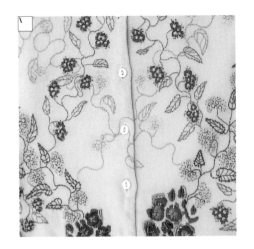

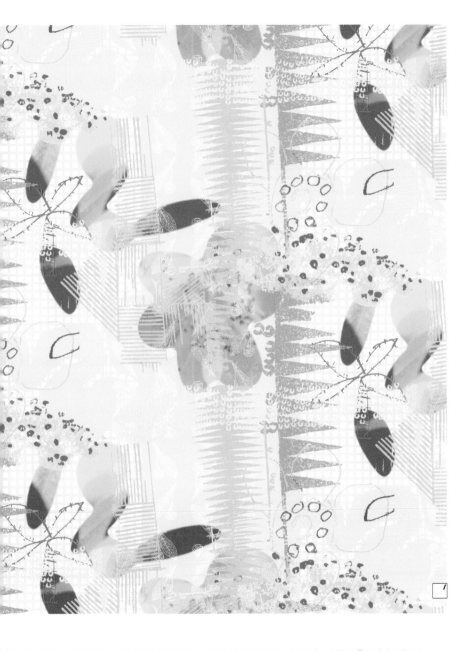

Annie Freud _ Meandering tendrils, leaves and delicate flowers have been hand embroidered on a woollen cardigan. The artist has this to say about it: 'My aim was to create a piece that communicated a sense of emblazoned queenliness undercut with nymphlike charm so as to emphasize the beauty of a woman's torso. Cotton, wool and gold thread have been used to create a symmetrical pattern.' **\\ Kim Barnett** _ Lazy blue daisies, purple flowers and red shoots form this design in a drawing style, which is whimsical without being twee. The artist comments: 'This is a design from a range based on fantasy flowers and plants. The strange little flowers are springing into the air, as if leaping for joy!' **/ Alex Russell** _ Floral drawings and photographs are layered with paintings inspired by traditional patterns in this very large design for fashion fabrics.

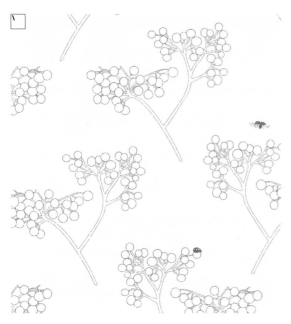

if only my children could go home...
but they haven't got wings!

\ **Andrew Hardiman** for **Kuboaa** _ The artist comments: 'A movement away from strong "feature wall" type papers, this was designed to be a less imposing paper, but one that continued to bring in a more fun element through the addition of flying ladybirds. Essentially I was trying to design a paper that those wishing to enter the new wallpaper fashion could access more easily.' \\ **Emily Burningham** _ The geese in this design look as though they have stepped out from a traditional folk tale with their crisp, stencilled outlines and bright red feet and beaks. \\\ **Dru Cole** _ Delicately drawn flowers are combined with heartshaped leaves in this fashion fabric. **/ Clare Perkins** _ The artist comments: 'This design was inspired by the Hungarian poem "The Dandelion's Tale" about a dandelion who was granted a wish by a fairy for her son and daughter to return to their homeland by being given wings.'

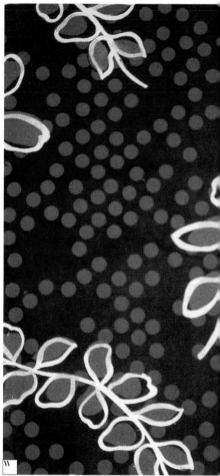

Alex Russell _ Silhouettes of seed heads hover over a background of considerably enlarged marks in this large format repeat for furnishings.
\ Charlotte Chamberlain _ Lilac spots and turquoise leaves are printed on a deep purple background in this screenprinted sample. A crisp outline of white delineates the shape of the foliage. / Alex Russell _ Brilliant multicoloured flowers appear to shimmer and dance against an out-of-focus background in this fashion fabric. The artist remarks: 'This is a mix of photographs and considerably enlarged marks in a large-scale repeat.'
/ Michèle Peary _ Luminous cockatoos and distorted jewelled fabric have been collaged together in a digitally manipulated design.

\

\\

Organic Patterns

Emily Burningham _ Ripe quince and white blossom are drawn in a naturalistic style recalling traditional floral fabrics in this design for paper products. **\\ Erin Warriner** _ Swallow shapes cut from grey lace meander upwards in this digital design. The artist comments: 'The inspiration for the bird images came from wildlife photographs taken in my local park. These were simplified and used as stencils, which were filled with a sample of lace before being digitally enhanced.' **/ Hanna Cottrell** _ Part of a series of designs exploring the complexities of Japanese paper folding, this design explores the contrast between the man-made forms and the delicate elements of the natural fauna and flora. **// Andrew Hardiman** for **Kuboaa** _ A detail from a large format wall covering showing a flattened stylized flower and leaf design printed in one colour – in this case aqua – on to cream.

Organic Patterns

Emily Burningham _ These boldly marching geese look as though they mean business. They make admirable guards and anyone who has been confronted by a gaggle of angry geese might hesitate before purchasing this design. **\\ Emily Burningham** _ Generously proportioned blossoms and leaves on a cool blue background evoke a feeling of the long lazy days of summertime. These pom-pom blooms are chrysanthemums, flowers that first became popular in the mid-nineteenth century, thanks to the influence of Japonism. **/ Julie Ingham** _ Directly inspired from the traditional art of paper cutting, this pattern combines Oriental style and Western style floral sprays, to produce a pattern that unites the two cultures. No small trick!

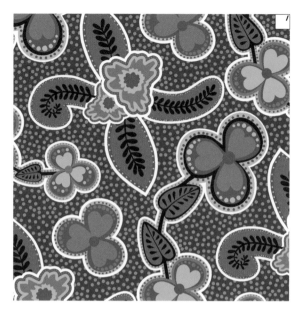

Michèle Peary _ Exotic flowers have been painted in brilliantly coloured inks in this large-scale pattern. The artist comments: 'I hand paint the flowers and let the dyes drip, then have them digitally printed and put on to canvas.' **/ Nadja Girod** _ Boldly rendered flower and leaf shapes are highly stylized to produce an allover design that is full of vitality. The artist comments: 'This fantasy print is a design I did for swimwear. Blue is one of the best-selling colours for swimwear and had to be included. Those are flowers I made up myself, thinking of summer, flowers, fruits and swimming pools.' **// Aj Dimarucot** for **Collision-Theory** _ Striped cherries and strawberries with bites out of them are arranged on a brilliant turquoise background in this fabric design. These fruits are a favourite choice for surface pattern designers, doubtless for the pleasant associations and happy memories they evoke.

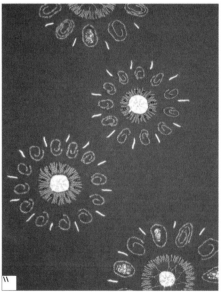

Organic Patterns

Gillian Tallentire _ This pattern is part of a series entitled 'Over the Garden Gate'. The artist comments: 'This colour combination works particularly well. I feel it has something of a three-dimensional effect and you could believe that things are happening just over the fence and down the hill!' **\\ Donna Bailey** _ Hand embroidered circles and spirals feature in this design intended for couture fashion fabrics. **\\\ Clare Perkins** _ This design was inspired by the flight of birds in an oversized garden and features appliqué details and machine embroidery. **/ Mary Daniel-Miller** _ Hibiscus flowers, made of collaged multicoloured images, create a design for wall coverings.

Organic Patterns

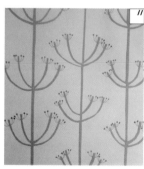

Clare Perkins _ Cherry blossom, origami birds and butterflies are combined to create a design that is unmistakably Japanese in its inspiration.
Clare Perkins _ Inspired by the work of the artist Darren Waterston, this design features magical islands, which have been hand painted on to silk. It was then screenprinted with fish and cherry blossom and appliquéd details added. **// Rachel Cave** _ Wonderfully bold and simple collaged shapes of upturned umbrella-like flower stalks rise up against a cyan sky, in this design for a furnishing fabric. **/// Gavin Horton** _ Humorous little birds flutter to and fro in this pattern. Their perky features convey a gentle ambience as well as one of whimsy. The artist comments: 'My work stems from childhood visits to my aunt's home. Her eclectic mixture of objects from every era gave me the inspiration to create designs of my own, with imagery that has a sense of humour and naïve charm, which evokes feelings of childhood fun.'

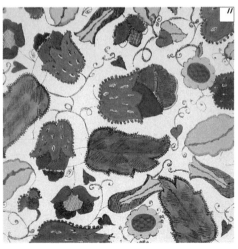

Michèle Peary _ Giant lime green spots form the background for these painted parrots. Blue feather-like shapes enhance the feeling of a tree top in a rain forest. \\ Rachel Cave _ Lime green shoots and leaves, together with olive green details, are set against a jade green background in this collaged design for a wall covering. / Jiwon Jahng _ Flowering Cacti have been printed on to silk satin in this fabric sample. // Dru Cole _ Raspberry and purple abstracted flowers are mixed with jade green and yellow leaves and delicately curling tracery in this design.

Kim Barnett _ Flowers and stems in shades of green form this deceptively simple design. On further inspection it can be seen that the flowers are composed of pieces of knitted fabrics. Knitting seems to play a major part in this designer's work – cropping up in collages and designs regularly see pages 36 and 46).

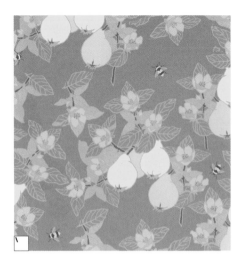

200 Organic Patterns

\ Emily Burningham _ Brightly coloured and carefully observed fruits and flowers of the quince tree, together with some stripy bees, make up this design. The whole scene is one of tranquillity and abundance. **\\ Hanna Werning** _ Combinations of flora and animals characterize this designer's artwork. The artist writes: 'One design is driven by ideas and another is more visual and driven by intuitive use of colours and rhythm. They can weave into each other.' **\\\ Hanna Werning** _ Zebras peer out from stylized plant forms in this 'Animal Flower' design for a wallpaper-poster. The large design repeats for use in an interior design situation. **/ Hanna Werning** _ Yellow leaves and turquoise foliage surround an elephant and a stag in this design for an 'Animal Flower' wallpaper-poster.

Organic Patterns

Hanna Werning _ Featuring seahorses and stencilled flowers, this pattern is part of the 'Animal Flower' series for wallpaper-posters. **/ Julie**
ngham _ Paisley patterns of leaves and flowers are layered with details in orange and pink in this digital design for textiles. The artist comments:
'This border design was created with summer in mind. I was trying to create a look that drew upon the traditional and yet is contemporary.'

\

\\

Organic Patterns

Julie Ingham _ Fronds and foliage were the original inspiration for this digitally created fashion fabric with its crisply delineated outlines.
Nathalie Pellon _ Lime green posies of flowers and herbs are suspended over concentric circles in this design entitled 'White Magic'. / Faizal
Reza for Skuitrgun _ Twisting and undulating organic forms feature in this pattern. The artist comments: 'The idea/style was conceived while I
was babysitting my one-year-old daughter. I was doodling on a piece of paper in front of her, with an ambitious thought of teaching her how to draw.
When I look back at the doodle, it just clicked that I could actually expand this. I guess it was part of the inner child in me that came up with this
style.'

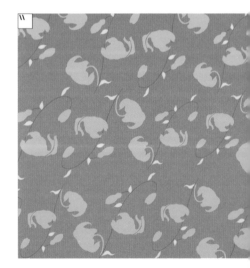

Grace Tabi _ Stylized cows, large and small, form this pattern. These cattle do not seem to fit the stereotypes of cuddly or cute animals, and are perhaps most likely to appeal to dairy farmers. **\\ Sandra Setyawan** _ Lime green leaves float across a muted background in a pattern that has the 'whiplash' forms characteristic of Art Nouveau designs of the early twentieth century. **/ Dru Cole** _ Pink roses burst out of this screenprinted textile, interspersed with delicately drawn scattered leaves. Florals continue to be the most popular print for textiles, and roses are particularly well loved. **// Emily Burningham** _ Orange fruit and leaves cascade down this design for gift wrap and greeting cards.

Alex Docker _ The layer effect in this design was inspired by the silhouettes of leaves found in woodlands around water. \\ **Alex Docker** _ A ock of gold, asymmetrically printed, adds interest to this pattern. The artist remarks: 'The gold leaf represents the sun's reflection creating shadows n the water's surface. Printed on to felt it gives the design a less fluid quality while complementing the clean edges and straight lines.' \\\ **Alex ocker** _ Delicately drawn dragonflies perch on fine green leaves against a background of burnished gold in this pattern. The artist comments: his soft interpretation of water's reflection depicts a tranquil summer's day by the water's edge, enhanced by the warm tones of green foliage.'
Andrew Hardiman for **Kuboaa** _ The artist says: 'Entitled 'Wisteria', this design is a visual translation of a well used plant in wallpaper, given an pdate. It was designed to spread across the wall in the same way that the plant does.'

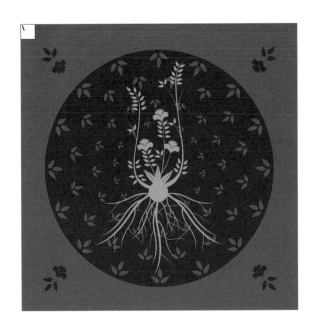

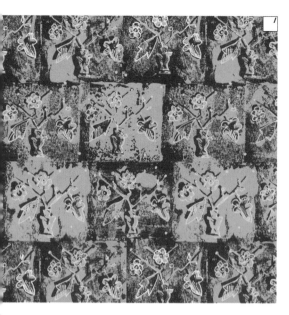

 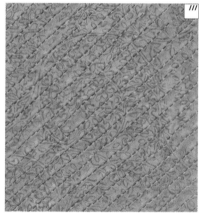

Daniele de Battè _ A light blue plant motif against a background of olive green features in this design for ceramic tiles. **\\ Timorous Beasties** _ Finely defined organic forms appear in this design, with an underlying shadow drawing of women apparently thumbing their noses at the viewers! **Dru Cole** _ Thorny stems and flowers in a vase are repeated across this pattern. Darker shadows play intermittently in the background, giving it a three-dimensional quality. **// Charlotte Chamberlain** _ Reminiscent of Art Nouveau designs, this fabric design features nasturtium leaves, which have been hand embroidered. **/// Sophie Gorton** _ A delicate tracery of leaves can just about be seen in this sample. The artist comments: 'My aim is to challenge the aesthetic of environmental design in textile and fashion. This piece is created using layers of recycled polyester fabric and plastic bottles made into fabric (PET). The leaf design has been applied with heat transfer and the "stitched" lines are welded ultrasonically, trapping a wadded layer between the PET fabrics.'

\ Emily Burningham _ Brilliant black fruits peep out from under long leaves, in this design entitled 'Oleaster'. The style is reminiscent of that of Art Nouveau artist Eugène Grasset, who stated that: 'Simply copying nature was not the way; rather, the artist needed to repeatedly accentuate colours and forms.' **\\ Lorien Huggins** _ Printed on to hand-dyed paper, these scrolling tendrils and flattened flowers draw inspiration from the celebrated Victorian designer William Morris. **\\\ Lorien Huggins** _ Orange polka dots form the background for a naturalistic depiction of a lily in this screenprinted fabric. Lilies were the quintessential flower of Art Nouveau designs and have retained their populairty. **/ Nadia Sparham** _ This spiralling pattern contains curling organic lines and bulbous orange pods and its repeat takes the eye on a journey around the swirling forms and into their hidden depths.

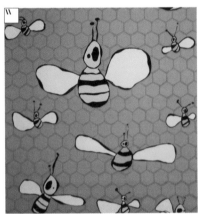

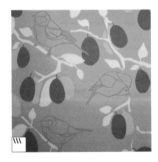

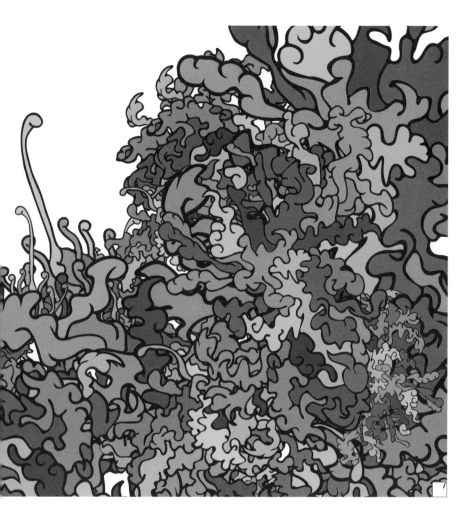

Andrew Hardiman for **Kuboaa** _ Entitled 'Bonsai', this is a large format wall covering, which shows leaves from a gingko or maidenhair tree. The artist writes: 'From studying some Japanese design, I wanted to do a simple Oriental pattern using the bonsai tree motif, but giving it a certain stylized quality.' **\\ Grace Tabi** _ Bees hovering over their honeycomb are portrayed in a flat, two-dimensional manner in this nursery fabric design. Each bee has been given its own character, adding to the playful effect. **\\\ Anna Ostrat** _ The delicacy of the birds' portrayal and their relationship with the boldness of the fruit makes this pattern memorable. **/ Faizal Reza** for **Skuirtgun** _ The rounded outlines in this design intertwine in a mass of connected shapes and there is a disturbing feeling of surging vitality, especially in the upright forms in the top left-hand corner.

\ **Alex Docker** _ The elegant shapes of these ferns and overhanging branches were directly inspired by Japanese decorative motifs. The artist comments: 'The metallic blue foil on this design produces a shimmer to recreate the properties of water while adding a shot of bright colour.'
\\ **Nadja Girod** _ This animal print is simply about each animal's favourite food. The bright yellow colour pulls the design together, and imbues it with a certain jolliness. The artist says: 'It is a kid's print and you can easily make up a story around it to entertain a kid when it is bored.' / **Carina Lago Gonzales** _ Inspired by images from microbiology, this pattern is of cells in concentric circles. // **Natalie Clay** _ The sketchy informal style of these flower drawings is offset by the careful portrayal of the red leaves that intersperse them.

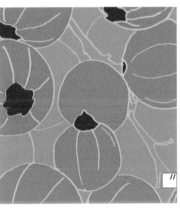

Andrew Hardiman for **Kuboaa** _ Sinuous stems combined with stylized flower heads feature in this wall covering. The textured detail of the stems, together with the stencil-like portrayal of the leaves and flowers, are shown to advantage by the spread and space of the white background. **Laura Vickers** _ Collaged flowers, trees and drawn stems and leaves are combined in this unusual design. The artist comments: 'I draw and collage until I find a composition that works on fabric. The drawn quality of my prints is what keeps them unique.' **// Emily Burningham** _ Scarlet fruits like over-inflated balloons are set against a background of lime green on this design for a greeting card. Scarlet and green were the signature colours of Coco Chanel and have been fashionable for a very long time.

220 Organic Patterns

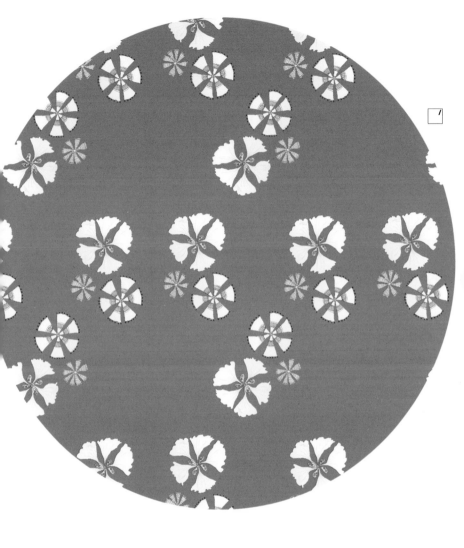

Peter Alexander Gomez _ This design incorporates different finishes such as glass and mica to give an almost three-dimensional effect. The burgundy coloured background forms a pattern as dynamic as that of the leaves, and it is this element that holds the pattern together and gives it such strength. \\ **Gavin Horton** _ The quality of this design is demonstrated by the sureness of touch in the execution of the flowers, their placing, their distance from each other and the relationship of the motifs and their dazzling white centres to the bright red background. \\\ **Gavin Horton** _ The artist comments: 'My work is the combination of clean lines and strong colour, which create fun designs that appeal to everyone. My aim is to create collections that will enliven any environment and are robust enough for children, yet exciting enough for the most forward-thinking adult consumer.' **/ Kim Barnett** _ Irregular petal shapes of the dianthus produce this pattern for a ceramic plate.

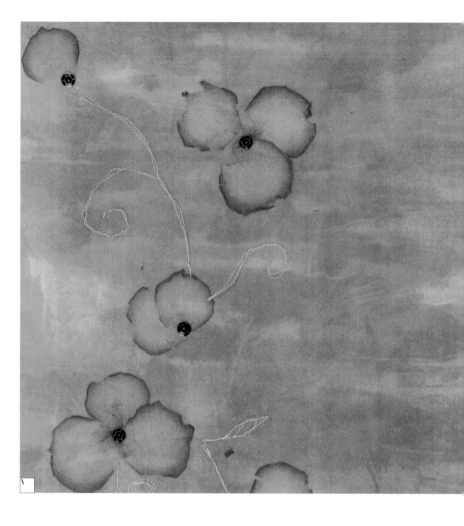

Cecilia Heffer _ In this fabric sample the real rose petals have been embellished by stitching and embroidery. The artist comments: 'This pattern was designed specifically as a placement print for women's wear. The idea was to create an ethereal feeling and sensitive colouring through subtle texture and finishing.' **/ Grace Tabi** _ The strange blue creatures in this pattern might well be bees – as they have honeycomb marks on their backs and wings. They hover rather menacingly over a few blades of grass in this neon pink coloured landscape. **// Andrew Hardiman** for **Kuboaa** _ Hummingbirds flutter around fuchsias in this design for a wall covering.

Organic Patterns

Michèle Peary _ Recycled paper cockatoos decorate a painting of exotic flowers that is reminiscent of large-scale designs called 'patio prints', hich were fashionable in the 1940s. **/ Charlotte Chamberlain** _ The muted colour palette in this hand screenprinted sample accentuates its semblance to the arborescent designs of the nineteenth century. **// Erin Warriner** _ Freesias in the shape of swallows have been collaged gether in a vertical arrangement in this wallpaper design. The artist comments: 'All my designs feature a mixture of both traditional and ontemporary trends in pattern, colour and imagery. In this design I used pressed flowers from my garden to put behind my hand cut stencils birds.'

Organic Patterns

Sarah Devey _ Sketchbook drawings of butterflies and an assortment of flora and fauna overlay patterns of paper doilies in this design. The artist remarks: 'Inspired by my caravan holidays by the seaside, this image is entitled "Doilies and Dreams" and recalls an afternoon eating cake and dreaming about tomorrow.' **/ Anna Ostrat** _ Nordic scenery has clearly inspired this luminous design of a winter landscape where half-hidden suns peep out from behind pale clouds and stark tree shapes. The palette of de-saturated mauves, pinks and burgundy is relieved by touches of scarlet and emphasized by the black of the birch trees.

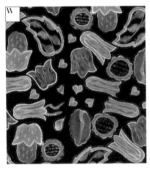

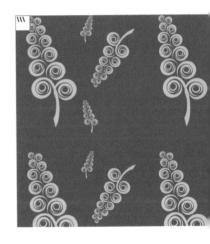

\ **Clare Perkins** _ This striking image of five koi carp swimming in a serene pool of mauve and violet has been created via a combination of hand painting, screenprinting and flocking. **\\ Dru Cole** _ Shimmering, organic shapes seem to vibrate like plankton in the depths of the sea in this fabric design. **\\\ Emantras-India** _ Pale mauve swirls, large and small, appear in this digital pattern. The artist comments: 'These spiralling trees are set on to a flat background and can be seen from any direction. The forms were inspired by roses, grapes and trees.' **/ Michèle Peary** _ An explosion of colours resembling the night sky during Bonfire Night is actually an Impressionistic design of flowers and birds executed using inks and coloured paper.

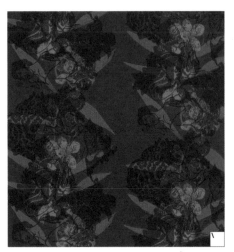

Organic Patterns

\ **Timorous Beasties** _ In this colourway of the 'Orchid' design, the mood is one of decadence and voluptuousness. The eerie figures half seen in the background take on more importance, and interact in a rather disturbing way with the brightly glowing magenta orchids and livid green leaves in the forefront. \\ **Emily Burningham** _ Entitled 'Delphiniums' the luminous mauves of the flowers and the jade green of the leaves contrast with the jet black of the background to create a neonlike effect. \\\ **Emily Burningham** _ This design portrays *magnolia grandiflora*, which has oversized, highly fragrant flowers. / **Emily Burningham** _ Stylized water lilies with delicate pink centres float serenely in this print designed for paper products. Their simplified forms suggest the influence of traditional Japanese textiles and prints.

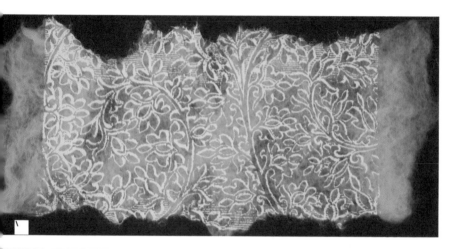

Organic Patterns

\ Sophie Gorton _ White felt is subtly printed with a lace design. The artist comments: 'By mixing traditional and modern techniques with both organic and recycled fabrics, I am creating original garments reminiscent of past treasures. This felt is handmade from waste wool from Italy, and is extremely fine and delicate. It is held together by the pigment print on the surface.' **\\ Emily Alston** _ Birds and leaves trail in deliberately emphasized diagonal lines in this wall covering. **/ Maria Yaschuk** _ If you look closely, you can just make out a tiny figure running through this design entitled 'Magic Forest'. The artist comments: 'This design is part of a collection which explores light through reflective materials. It also challenges the shape of the roll and the linear way we apply wallpaper to the wall surface.'

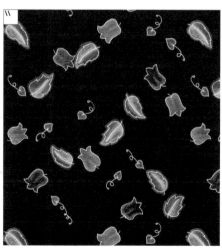

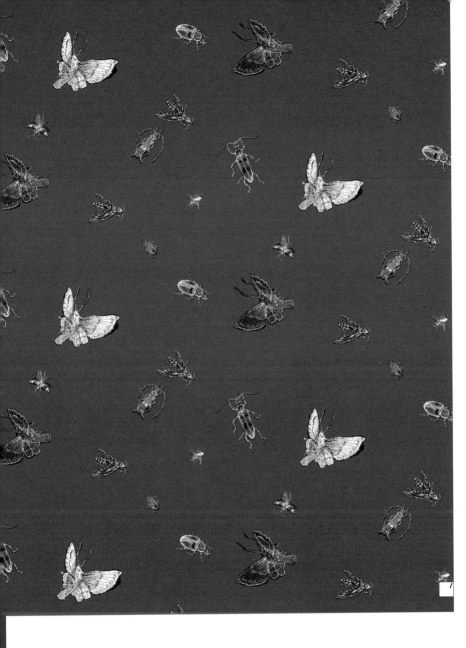

\ **Annie Freud** _ Meandering leaf and stem shapes have been hand embroidered on to black cashmere. The artist comments: 'This design was inspired by a paisley dress in a painting by my father of my grandmother. I have tried to make the motifs appear like living organisms.' \\ **Dru Cole** _ Leaves and flower shapes fall across a black background in a cascade of delicate colour in this fabric design. \\\ **Lorien Huggins** _ Reminiscent of Art Nouveau designs, these delicate tendrils and flattened flower heads have been hand screenprinted in silver and grey on to silk satin. / **Timorous Beasties** _ Meticulously drawn butterflies and beetles are pinned to the inky blackness of their surroundings in this disquieting design. This design team delight in the inclusion of unsettling and disconcerting details in their patterns.

Organic Patterns

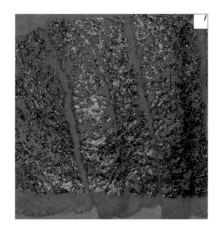

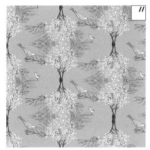

\ Keira March _ This handwoven fabric sample uses hand-dyed, spun silk yarns. The artist comments: 'I wove the cloth to have areas of violet over the warm black background. Then, to create even more texture, I chose to hand stitch sequins on top, to appear almost like flies caught within a spider's web.' **/ Sophie Gorton** _ Gold foiling has been printed on to this piece of handmade felt. The artist comments: 'By combining laser, emboss, stitch, shibori and shrink with print I aim to suggest traditions such as lace, embroidery, quilting and smocking.' **// Hanna Cottrell** _ The artist remarks: 'I am interested in how digital techniques merged with traditional mark making methods can work alongside each other to create a collection of fresh and interesting ideas.' **/// Hanna Cottrell** _ Naturalistically portrayed birds and branches create an unusual and complex design for wallpaper. The artist comments: 'Drawing forms a huge part of my work and I exploit my personal drawing style to emphasize my own individual design signature.'

CONTRIBUTORS

Emily Anderson
discodolly84@hotmail.com

Sarah Angold
sarahangold@hotmail.com

Emily Alston
emily@emilyforgot.co.uk

Savaine Auzende for Mekanism
fred2radikal@cegetel.net

Els Van Baarle
elsvanbaarle@zeelandnet.nl

Donna Bailey
donnabailey45@hotmail.com

Kim Barnett
birds.in.skirts@gmail.com

Johanna Basford
johanna_b_2000@yahoo.com

Daniele de Battè
danieledebatte@libero.it

Timorous Beasties
info@timorousbeasties.com

Naomi Bolt
naomi_bolt@yahoo.co.uk

Denise Boyle
info@babyd.co.uk

Karen Bravo
karenmariebravo@yahoo.com

Emily Burningham
info@emilyburningham.com

Marc Burton
mrmarcburton@hotmail.com

Rachel Cave
rachelcave1@hotmail.com

Giovanna Cellini
gio.cellini@virgin.net

Charlotte Chamberlain
charlotte_chamberlain1@hotmail.com

Church of London
iamwilloughby@gmail.com

Natalie Clay
nataliecornwall@yahoo.com

Dominic Crinson
info@crinson.com

Dru Cole
www.drusillacole.co.uk / druvcole@aol.com

Peggy Cole
peggycarey255@gmail.com

Naja Conrad-Hansen
najaconrad@aab11.dk

Lena Corwin
lena@lenacorwin.com

Hanna Cottrell
dodos_frighten_me@hotmail.com

Mary Daniel-Miller
pheebs39@hotmail.com

Delaware
mail@delaware.gr.jp

Sarah Devey
sarah.devey@RCA.ac.uk

Aj Dimarucot for Collision-Theory
adj@collision-theory.com

Alex Docker
alexkdocker@aol.com

Alex Eddison
helloalexeddison@yahoo.co.uk

Carlene Edwards
carlene.edwards@btinternet.com

Emantras-india
charanya@emantras.com

Jiri Evenhuis for Materialise.MGX
info@materialise.be

Annie Freud
freud@dircon.co.uk

Nadja Girod
hello@nadjagirod.com

Peter Alexander Gomez
peteralexandergomez@gmail.com

Carina Lago Gonzales
carina_lago@hotmail.com

Emma Gray
e_gray_2000@yahoo.com

Bathsheba Grossman for Materialise.MGX
info@materialise.be

Sophie Gorton
sophie@sophiegorton.com

Victoria Graham
vicky_k_graham@yahoo.co.uk

Louise Gullick
lougullick@yahoo.co.uk

Marie Hansen
hello@ordinarymary.dk

Stefan Hanser
info@visuelle-systeme.de

Andrew Hardiman for Kuboaa
info@kuboaa.co.uk

Cecilia Heffer
cecilia.heffer@uts.edu.au

Pauline Holt for Jazzy Lily Hot Glass
pauline@jazzylily.freeserve.co.uk

Gavin Horton
thehortons_ebne@tinyworld.co.uk

Lorien Huggins
lorienm.huggins@virgin.net

Julie Ingham
julieingham@btconnect.com

Jiwon Jahng
tigertigerlillyuk@yahoo.com

Yerin Jeon
yerin@hotmail.com

Ed Jones
drgonzo458@hotmail.com

Marloes Jongen
loesjeloes@hotmail.com

Louise Kallinicou
louisekallinicou@hotmail.com

Petra Kather
katherp@gmx.de

Joanna Kinnersley-Taylor
joanna.k-t@virgin.net

Michelle Lucas
shell_220@fsmail.net

Keira March
keiramarch@hotmail.com

Caroline Mcnamara
cmcna12@aol.com

Dominic Meaker
snootens@hotmail.com

Rachel Moore
rachey1982@hotmail.com

Kristina Mörsdorf
wesenchen@hotmail.com

Sally-Ann Murphy
dottydesigns@aol.com

Anna Ostrat
annaostrat@hotmail.com

Michelè Peary
shell_13uk@yahoo.co.uk

James Pegg
jpeggdesigns@aol.com

Nathalie Pellon
sciri@friends.bbb.ch

Clare Perkins
clareyperkins@yahoo.co.uk

Gina Pipet
ginapipet1@hotmail.co.uk

Veronica Pock
veronica_pock@hotmail.com

Heather Power
heatherpower@hotmail.co.uk

Vivien Prideaux
priddypink@macace.co.uk

Naori Priestly
naori@priestly.plus.com

Eleanor Pritchard
eleanorpritchard@lycos.co.uk

Faizal Reza for Skuirtgun
skuirt9un@gmail.com

Alex Russell
alex@alexrussell.com

Suse Schröder
australiensuse@gmx.de

Sandra Setyawan
sandrasetyawan@gmail.com

Nadia Sparham
nadiussparhythe@hotmail.com

Janet Stoyel for clothclinic.com
info@clothclinic.com

Marina Strumphler
marinas@dutchtextiledesign.com

Sara Sulemanji
sarasul99@hotmail.com

Grace Tabi
eyesbrowng@hotmail.com

Safa Maryam Taheri
moo_ju_@hotmail.com

Gillian Tallentire
gilliantallentire@hotmail.com

Rachael Taylor
glitterfairychic@hotmail.com

Ben Trill for Interim.org.uk
info@interim.org.uk

Peter Uertz
peter@uertz.de

Eugene van Veldhoven
eugene@dutchtextiledesign.com

Laura Vickers
vickerslaura40@aol.com

Erin Warriner
erinwarriner@yahoo.co.uk

Hanna Werning
hello@byhanna.com

Frans Wesselman
frans@wesselman.freeserve.co.uk

Sue Westergaard
suewestergaard@msn.com

Darren Wilkinson Mawer
drwm1@hotmail.com

Gavin Wilshen
eyeidsign@yahoo.com

Jessie Whipple
cameron@kunstkraft.com

Maria Yaschuk
maria_yaschuk@yahoo.com

BIBLIOGRAPHY

Bosker, Gideon, M. Mancini, and J. Gramstad, *Fabulous Fabrics of the 50s*, Chronicle Books, San Francisco, 1992

Box, Richard, *Colour and Design for Embroidery*, Batsford, London, 2000

Brito, Karren K., *Shibori*, Watson-Guptill Publications, New York, 2002

Butts, Robert, *The Early Sessions*, New Awareness Network Inc., New York, 2005

Cole, Emily, *The Grammar of Architecture*, Bullfinch Press, Boston, 2002

Cole, Drusilla, *1000 Patterns*, A&C Black, London, 2003

Conran, Terence, *Printed Textile Design*, Studio Publications, London, 1957

Deschodt, Anne-Marie, *Fortuny*, Harry N. Abrams, New York, 2001

Day, Lewis F., *Pattern Design*, General Publishing Co., Toronto, 1999

Durant, Stuart, *Ornament*, The Overlock Press, New York, 1986

Edwards, Betty, *Color*, Tarcher/Penguin, New York, 2004

Fiell, Charlotte, and Peter Fiell, *50s Decorative Art*, Taschen, Köln, 2000

Fukai, A., et al, *Fashion: A History from the 18th to the 20th Century*, Taschen, Kyoto, 2005

Haslam, Marion, *Retro Style*, Cassell & Co., London, 2000

Hoskins, Lesley, *The Papered Wall*, Thames and Hudson, London, 1994

Jackson, Lesley, *The New Look: Design in the Fifties*, Thames & Hudson, London, 1998

Jenkyn Jones, Sue, *Fashion Design*, Laurence King Publishing, London, 2002

Joyce, Carol, *Textile Design*, Watson-Guptill Publications, New York, 1993

McNamara Andrea, and Patrick Snelling, *Design and Practice for Printed Textiles*, Oxford University Press, Melbourne, 2000

Mellor, S., and J. Elffers, *Textile Designs*, Thames & Hudson, London, 1991

Raynor, G., R. Chamberlain, and A. Stapleton, *Artists' Textiles in Britain 1945–1970*, Antique Collector's Club, London, 2003

Saito, Ryukyu, *Japanese Ink-Painting: Lessons in Suiboko Techniques*, Kodasha International, London, 1965

Schoeser, Mary, and Celia Rufey, *English and American Textiles*, Thames & Hudson, New York, 1989

Tanenbaum, Carole, *Vintage Costume Jewellery*, Antique Collector's Club, Woodbridge, 2006

Yusuf, Nilgin, *Georgina von Etzdorf*, Thames & Hudson, London, 1998